THE POWER OF HIS PRESENCE

To my precious daughter we will love you forever.

THE
POWER
OF HIS
PRESENCE

✧

Adrian Rogers

Innovo Publishing LLC
www.innovopublishing.com
1-888-546-2111

Providing Full-Service Publishing Services for
Christian Authors, Artists, and Organizations: Hardbacks, Paperbacks,
eBooks, Audiobooks, Music, and Film

THE POWER OF HIS PRESENCE

Unless otherwise indicated, Bible quotations are taken from the King James Version.

Library of Congress Control Number: 2015937137
ISBN 13: 978-1-61314-264-6

Interior Layout & Cover Design by Innovo Publishing LLC
and Eternity Communications

Printed in the United States of America
U.S. Printing History
Second Edition: May 2015

To Joyce

godly wife and mother,
cherished sweetheart,
wise counselor,
and
best friend

Table of Contents

Preface

Real salvation is not getting man out of earth into heaven, but getting God out of heaven into man. That seems like a simple truth. So why did it take me so long to know it?

It is not that God has willingly hidden these things. Yet, as a young Christian I was evidently blinded to a discoverable secret that literally saturates the Word of God.

I came to Christ for salvation as a teenager. I meant every word of it when I gave my heart to Christ. My young heart was filled with zeal and a love for the things of God. At that time, I gave all I knew of me to all I knew of Him.

Yet there was little victory in my daily walk. My small blips of overcoming and victorious living were rare moments in my continuing struggle. Raging hormones, a combative personality, and an untamed tongue were tools I placed in Satan's hand to build a prison house of failure for me. It seemed that I lived there most of my days.

By the grace of God, I managed to hold on, to keep myself sexually pure and away from the more vile and open sins, but my life could not be described as victory.

Every so often I would venture from my prison house of failure. I would rededicate my life and make promises. Now I had a fresh start. I would do better. But resolve, resolution, and repentance were not enough.

I was sincere when I said I wanted to do better. I promised I would try harder. I had learned determination on the football field, and I thought perhaps I could "gut it out" in my Christian life. But before many days or even hours had passed, I had failed again. Back to the dungeon!

If I had only learned then what I know now. There is only One Who has ever lived the Christian life. His name is Jesus. If the Christian life is being lived through you, it indeed is not you but Christ who lives in you:

> I am crucified with Christ: nevertheless I live; yet not I, but Christ liveth in me: and the life which I now live in the flesh I live by the faith of the Son of God, who loved me, and gave himself for me (Galatians 2:20).

Indeed, of all of the truths that I have finally learned, I do not know of one that is more encouraging and life changing than the marvelous and vital truth that God is alive and well in me through His Son, Jesus Christ.

Yet it is possible to be a Christian like I was and not be aware of this. Paul had to remind the believers at Corinth, "What? know ye not that your body is the temple of the Holy Ghost which is in you, which ye have of God, and ye are not your own?" (1 Corinthians 6:19). He reminded them again in 2 Corinthians 6:16, "Ye are the temple of the living God; as God hath said, 'I will dwell in them, and walk in them; and I will be their God, and they shall be my people.'"

It may take us this lifetime and into eternity to finally understand and grasp all that this means, but I know this: God meant it to be a bright, living reality in our daily lives! God wants to change the mundane into the momentous and drudgery into delight. He wants to turn struggle into victory.

So in these pages I want to explore with you some implications, applications, and, yes, some common misunderstandings of what it means to have God inhabit your humanity and make you a dwelling place with a Royal Resident.

I have not arrived, but these truths are helping me move on to maturity and victory. And I am eager to share with you what the Holy Spirit is teaching me.

In our journey together we will touch on theology and some very important doctrines, but I want to give you a word of caution. I have learned that one can know theology and still not experience the power of God. And I also know beyond a doubt that one can experience Christ without a full understanding of Christian theology. Thankfully, we don't have to choose between the two. Sound doctrine and holy living make up the norm for a victorious Christian.

One of God's great ways of communicating spiritual truth so it is easily understood is by use of illustrations. The Bible abounds with these. Jesus used illustrations over and over as He taught. The vine and the branches, a farmer's field, and a pearl are but a few examples.

One of the clearest illustrations and object lessons of spiritual truth is the Old Testament temple. This magnificent building, constructed according to a precise pattern, was given by the Master Teacher to help us grasp spiritual truth. Therefore, as we consider our experience of Christ, we will begin with the truths taught by the Old Testament temple.

Not to worry. We are not going to embark on a complicated study of the intricate details of the temple. Nor will we go down long and come up dry theologically. As you will see, our study is really about you and the victory that God has provided for you.

In the Old Testament, God had a temple for His people. In the New Testament, He had a people for His temple. Our very bodies are holy temples. And the Lord Himself is the Royal Resident who lives within us. What a staggering thought!

This truth of the fullness of the indwelling God is so very vital and valuable to each one of us. There is no greater truth than to discover that the great God of glory has condescended to indwell mortals such as we. No wonder Paul wrote, "Christ in you, the hope of glory" (Colossians 1:27).

I pray that these words will become a bright, living reality in you and that you will discover the key that unlocks the treasure house of a thousand other spiritual riches. Drabness and discouragement can be a thing of the past. You are a residence of the living God! Living supernaturally is the most natural thing a Christian can do.

CHAPTER ONE

Where on Earth Does God Live?

In order to understand and apply all of the benefits of Christ's indwelling presence, I want to begin where God began revealing the truth that He would dwell among His people. That beginning point is God's instructions to Moses. The Lord came to Moses and told him to have the children of Israel bring Him an offering for the building of the tabernacle, "that I may dwell among them" (Exodus 25:8).

Don't miss the importance of what God said. The great God of creation, the God who inhabits eternity, wanted a place to dwell among His people! No, the tabernacle could not contain the infinite God, any more than the temple could. But this sanctuary, which was later made permanent in the temple, was the one place on earth where God would meet with His people for instruction, worship, blessing, and atonement for sin.

You can really see the importance of this dwelling in Exodus 29:45, where God said, "I will dwell among the children of Israel, and will be their God." But wait a minute. Was He not Israel's God before this? Yes, He was, but the construction of the tabernacle/temple would mark a new day in God's relationship with His people. This structure would be a visible, daily reminder of His presence—and, more importantly, of His rightful place in the people's lives.

Calling out a people to be His dwelling-place on earth was God's purpose from the beginning. He made that clear in Exodus 29:46:

> And they shall know that I am the LORD their God, that brought them forth out of the land of Egypt, *that I may dwell among them*: I am the LORD their God (italics added).

As the late Bible scholar and professor Dr. Merrill Unger observed, "The tabernacle and all that pertained to it was typical of the presence of God with His people."[1]

Since the tabernacle was a prototype for the temple that would come later, it is important to remember God's command to Moses concerning the building of the tabernacle:

> According to all that I shew thee, after the pattern of the tabernacle, and the pattern of all the instruments thereof, even so shall ye make it (Exodus 25:9).

A House for God

Many centuries after Moses, when Israel was safe and secure in the land, God put the desire in King David's heart to replace the tabernacle with a more permanent building in Jerusalem, a place where God would continue to dwell among His people. As we know, David was prohibited from actually building the structure, an honor that fell to his son Solomon.

This new building was called "the temple," but it is interesting that it was often referred to as God's "house," a place of settled habitation.[2] Don't miss the point: *each stage of God's habitation among His people was more permanent than the one that preceded it.*

Since Paul called you and me temples of the Holy Spirit, let's look more closely at the Old Testament temple. I said this would not be an intricate study of the temple's details because that is not our purpose here. Rather, I want to take you on a brief walk around and through the temple.

When God designed the Old Testament temple, He designed it with the same three major parts or sections that the tabernacle contained. It is here that we get to the heart of our study because the three-fold pattern of the temple teaches us something very important about the nature of our God and about us as His temples in this age.

If we could walk up to that great temple of Solomon's, we would see the first section, the outer court, which was visible to all and visited by all. It was here in the outer court that external worship took place.

Next, and further in, was the holy place. This was a more restricted place where only the priests could go for worship and service to God.

Last, there was the holy of holies. This was the innermost court, absolutely off-limits except for the high priest, who was a prefiguring of Jesus. The high priest would enter the holy of holies once a year to make atonement for the people. It was here that God dwelt in His *shekinah* glory between the cherubim that covered the mercy seat of the ark of the covenant.

A House of Three Rooms

This house of three rooms conformed to a precise pattern. We have already seen that God commanded Moses to be very precise about the original design for the tabernacle. Note also the detailed directions given by David to Solomon for the construction of the temple:

> Then David gave to Solomon his son the pattern of the porch, and of the houses thereof, and of the treasuries thereof, and of the upper chambers thereof, and of the inner parlours thereof, and of the place of the mercy seat. And the pattern of all that he had by the spirit, of the courts of the house of the LORD, and of all the chambers round about, of the treasuries of the house of God, and of the treasuries of the dedicated things (1 Chronicles 28:11–12).

Then the Bible says, "All this, said David, the LORD made me understand in writing by his hand upon me, even all the works of this pattern" (v. 19). The reason for all this precision is that the tabernacle and the temple were to be grand object lessons. They were to teach us something of the nature of God and the nature of man.

One reason for this grouping into three areas is that the God we know and worship is a triune Being, one God in three distinct Persons—Father, Son, and Holy Spirit.

In fact, as we look at the world around us, we can see how all that God has created reflects the Holy Trinity in some way. For example, all space is triune in dimension: height, width, and depth. Each dimension is distinct from the other two, and yet all three are a part of the same, and no part exists without the other.

The same thing is true of time. Time is triune: past, present, and future. We cannot even imagine one element of time without the other two, and yet the three are always distinct from each other. Together these three components make up one basic entity—time.

Obviously, no illustration can adequately explain the Holy Trinity. Scholars have raced their theological motors to try and find an adequate, rational illustration of the Trinity. But all examples break down somewhere, and I am glad they do! The one true God—Father, Son, and Holy Spirit—is unique. Therefore, God cannot be truly compared to, or illustrated by, anything. We can only know the truth of the Trinity by revelation. "To whom then will ye liken me, or shall I be equal? saith the Holy One" (Isaiah 40:25).

Man: A Royal Residence

The truth of the Holy Trinity is certainly one of the mysteries of the faith. However, it is important to remind ourselves of God's triune nature because as the highest expression of His creation, we reflect His nature. If we are going to appreciate and appropriate all that it means to be the temples of the living God, we need to understand more about man's makeup.

The threefold nature of man is seen in 1 Thessalonians 5:23, where Paul wrote: "And the very God of peace sanctify you wholly; and I pray God your whole *spirit and soul and body* be preserved blameless unto the coming of our Lord Jesus Christ" (italics added).

Since we know from 1 Corinthians 6:19 that the Christian is God's temple, God's house, we can see how the Old Testament temple—with its three distinct but related parts—illustrates the New Testament truth of man's triune nature. Borrowing the imagery of the temple as God's house, it could be said that we are a house of three rooms.

17

I am aware that some theologians prefer to think of man as a dichotomy, as having only two parts to his nature: the body as the material part, and the soul and the spirit lumped together as the immaterial part. There is some truth to this approach because we are definitely both material and immaterial. But the Bible still speaks clearly of spirit, soul, and body. The spirit and soul may never be separated, and they do not operate independently of each other, but they certainly may be differentiated.

I believe that human nature consists of three parts because we are created to know three worlds: the spiritual world, the psychological world, and the material or physical world. Roughly speaking, we can think of these as the world above us, the world within us, and the world beneath us.

These three worlds are related to the three parts of our human nature—spirit, soul, and body. Understand this and many wonderful truths will come into focus. When a man is rightly related to the material world with his body, he is healthy. When he is rightly related to the psychological world with his soul, he is happy. When he is properly related to the spiritual world with his spirit, he is holy.

God's aim is that ultimately we are to experience all three realities: health, happiness, and holiness.

The Outer Man and the Material World

The body is what the Bible calls the "outward man" (2 Corinthians 4:16). The human body corresponds to the outer part of the Old Testament temple. That outer court of the temple was the place of sacrifice and, interestingly, our bodies are also the place of sacrifice. Paul commanded us to present our bodies as "a living sacrifice" (Romans 12:1).

18

It is not, by the way, true Christian thought to view the body as sinful or evil. The body is God's creation and should be presented to Him as a holy temple. Most of us need to realize this and do a better job of temple maintenance!

Yet, we do not need to buy into this fitness and fashion craze that overestimates the importance of the body. It is not your body, as we will see shortly, that gives you supreme value. Animals also have bodies, and so do vegetables. But man is much more than a toad or a turnip.

The Inner Man and the Psychological World

The soul is a bit more difficult for us to understand, if for no other reason than that it is invisible. Generally speaking we could say that the soul is the psychological part of our nature or human personality that lives in our body or "earthly house."

The Greek word for *soul* is *psyche*. This is the word from which we get *psychic*, *psychology*, and related words. The Bible seems to indicate that the soul consists primarily of our mind, emotions, and will. God's Word illustrates and catalogs the activities of the soul quite carefully.

For example, the soul is centered in the mind. "So shall the knowledge of wisdom be unto thy soul: when thou hast found it, then there shall be a reward, and thy expectation shall not be cut off" (Proverbs 24:14).

The soul is also the center of our emotions. "And it came to pass, when he had made an end of speaking unto Saul, that the soul of Jonathan was knit with the soul of David, and Jonathan loved him as his own soul" (1 Samuel 18:1).

Finally, the soul is the center of the will. "The things that my soul refused to touch are as my sorrowful meat" (Job 6:7).

We must not think of the soul as being inherently evil or irredeemable. Mind, emotion, and will are only evil as they have been corrupted through sin. The soul itself was created by God that through it we might understand Him, love Him, and serve Him. Thus, when we turn to the Lord, we are never called to crush or suppress our minds or wills or even our emotions. Instead, our souls (as do our bodies and spirits) come into union with Christ. As David says of the Lord, "He restoreth my soul" (Psalm 23:3).

The soul is also that part of our nature through which we relate to ourselves and others. My soul is the real me living inside my "earthly house." When you look at me, all you can really see is the "house" or body that I live in. This truth reminds me of former president Woodrow Wilson's favorite limerick, which went like this:

I know how ugly I are,
I know my face ain't no star,
But I don't mind it,
'Cause I'm behind it;
It's the fellow in front
Who gets the jar.

The Innermost Man and the Spiritual World

The human spirit, in the biblical sense of the word, is a mystery. What I mean is that it could never be discovered by human ingenuity. We know that man has a spirit only through the revelation of God's two-edged Sword. There is no surgeon's scalpel sharp enough to separate the human spirit from the soul; only the living Word of God can do that.

For the word of God is quick, and powerful, and sharper than any two-edged sword, piercing even to the dividing asunder of soul and spirit, and of the joints and marrow, and is a discerner of the thoughts and intents of the heart (Hebrews 4:12).

The uniqueness of man is seen in that he has a spirit. Animals certainly have bodies, and they can be said to have a soulish life, but they are void of spirit.

The Bible describes the creation of the animals in this way:

And God said, Let the earth bring forth the living creature after his kind, cattle, and creeping thing, and beast of the earth after his kind: and it was so (Genesis 1:24).

The Hebrew word translated "creature" in this verse is *nephesh*, which is usually translated "soul." It means self-conscious life, as opposed to plant life, which is without soul or spirit.

Plants and animals have bodies. Animals also have souls. But when God made man, He breathed into him "the breath of life" (Genesis 2:7). This "breath of life" became the human spirit, for the words *breath* and *spirit* are used interchangeably in the Bible. Man was endowed with a spiritual nature and thus the glorious ability to know and worship God. God did not breathe this special breath of life into any other of His creatures.

So note again, this is why the apostle wrote as he did in 1 Thessalonians 5:23, mentioning the three distinct parts of human nature as he prayed for believers.

If the human spirit is unique in all of creation, we need to ask, what is its function? We have already said it is the part of our nature that enables us to know and worship God. Mary said, "My spirit hath rejoiced in God my Saviour" (Luke 1:47).

Jesus told the woman at the well, "But the hour cometh, and now is, when the true worshippers shall worship the Father in spirit and in truth: for the Father seeketh such to worship him" (John 4:23). And Paul wrote, "The Spirit itself beareth witness with our spirit, that we are the children of God" (Romans 8:16).

Can Dogs Pray?

Animals will never pray, never seek God, and never worship because they have no spirit. That which keeps man from being more than a clever animal, with the ability to talk and walk upright, is his spirit. That which brings dignity to the soul of man—making it worth more than the whole wide world—is that it is inseparably linked to his spirit.

The soul of an animal will perish, but man's soul, eternally linked with his spirit, will live forever. It is endless, timeless, and dateless. One man or woman is worth more than all of the world because man, through his spirit, can know and worship and enjoy God.

How to Function with Unction

Understanding the human spirit is crucial to understanding what it means to have Christ living in us. The Bible describes the human spirit as a lamp. "The spirit of man is the candle of the LORD, searching all the inward parts of the belly" (Proverbs 20:27).

The word "candle" here is better translated as "lamp." A candle burns its own substance, but a lamp must be fed with oil. The oil that feeds the lamp of the human spirit is the Holy Spirit. Thus, we are given illumination through the power of the Holy Spirit working in our human spirit.

God the Father's intention for you and me is that we be joined to Christ so that the Holy Spirit can illuminate or enlighten our human spirit. Then our human spirit is meant to communicate God's divine will to our soul (the mind, emotions, and will), and the soul is meant to motivate the body to navigate out into the world with the purpose of accomplishing God's will.

We can see once again how the working of our spirit correlates with the Old Testament temple. Just as in the temple, God's presence was most directly manifested in the innermost room, the holy of holies, so in our human temples the innermost room, the spirit, is where the very presence of God should dwell with all of His fullness.

But the holy of holies did not stand alone. Neither does our spirit exist alone. It takes body, soul, and spirit working together to make us what the New Testament calls a temple of the living God, a place where He dwells.

When we yield to Christ, the will and the power of the invisible God will be made visible through our bodies, we will be at peace in our souls, and we will know the fullness of God's indwelling presence in our spirits. Then our invisible God will receive the glory due His name.

Jesus put it this way: "Let your light so shine before men, that they may see your good works, and glorify your Father which is in heaven" (Matthew 5:16).

At this point, I need to remind you that it is possible to misuse God's temple. The Jews were doing it in Jesus' day. They had taken charge of the temple, using it as a marketplace

23

to make a profit. Jesus had to drive out the moneychangers and take control of His temple once again. We can make the same error when we try to take back control of our lives. But instead of fashioning a whip, Jesus uses the prodding of the Holy Spirit to call us back to yieldedness before Him.

Is He There?

As a house of three rooms, the Old Testament temple illustrates the fact that man also is a house of three rooms. Does the great God live in your house? If He does, you have this promise: "For thus saith the high and lofty One that inhabiteth eternity, whose name is Holy; I dwell in the high and holy place, with him also that is of a contrite and humble spirit, to revive the spirit of the humble, and to revive the heart of the contrite ones" (Isaiah 57:15).

Ian Thomas has put it so well:

> To be in Christ—that is redemption; but for Christ to be in you—that is sanctification! To be in Christ—that makes you fit for heaven; but for Christ to be in you—that makes you fit for earth! To be in Christ—that changes your destination; but for Christ to be in you—that changes your destiny! The one makes heaven your home—the other makes this world His workshop.[3]

CHAPTER TWO

Supernaturally Natural,
Naturally Supernatural

One of the curses of twentieth-century Christianity is Sunday-morning religion:

> *They're praising God on Sunday,*
> *They'll be all right on Monday,*
> *It's just a little habit they've acquired.*

This is the problem of a house and a heart divided.

Have you ever been in a church service where people act "spiritual"? They get a stained-glass look on their faces and speak in funeral-home tones. Even the minister, who seems normal enough at the church picnic, stands in the pulpit and intones "dearly beloved" as if he'd just swallowed the Communion rail.

Yet, when the service is over and this sanctified throng reaches the cafeteria line over at the shopping center, they seem to be amazingly normal people. They have changed from the spiritual mode to the secular mode like someone has thrown a switch. The entire idea seems artificial, does it not?

The Sacred and the Secular

How do people acquire this "little habit" of worshiping God in church on Sunday and then reverting to their normal behavior when they pass through the doors? It's because they have bought the common idea that life is divided into the sacred and the secular. We leave the secular world outside when we go into a church to worship. Then, because we are in church, we suddenly begin acting like someone we're not. We keep the mask on for the worship hour, then lay it aside and head to the cafeteria line as if nothing had happened.

Let me pose an interesting question. What would happen to people like this if they had to spend all of their time in church? Working in the church, eating there, raising their families there, living there. Do you think their behavior would change? Would they act pious all the time because they were suddenly aware of being in God's presence in His house?

Yes, I know it's impossible to live at church. But as temples of the Holy Spirit, we do live in God's presence in His house. We *are* His house! We're not meant to be victims of "Sunday-morning religion." We are meant to be living sixty minutes an hour, twenty-four hours a day, three hundred and sixty-five days a year in the Spirit, worshiping and serving the Lord.

The sign over the church door where I attended as a boy said, "The Lord is in His holy temple. Let all of the earth keep silence." I mistakenly took that to mean that I had just entered the holy temple and had better start acting religious. How I wish that someone had taught me that the wonderful place I loved was not a temple of God, but that we, His people, are. Of course, we are to be reverent in a church service and should respect the place where we are meeting, but that is not the point at all.

The point is that as a Christian I needed to learn that I could not neatly divide my life into two divisions—the secular and the sacred. But when we restrict God's presence to a locality—the church on the corner, for example—that's what happens. And so we hear people say things like, "Politics and religion don't mix." "Faith is a private matter." "You don't understand . . . this is business!"

Well, it may be business, but it isn't biblical! Because we are indwelt by the Holy Spirit, the line between the secular and the sacred in our lives is erased. We do not need to "act" spiritual. We are spiritual. We are the temples of God on a full-time basis. Therefore, responding to life spiritually should be the most natural thing for us! Because the sign over our hearts reads, "A temple of God," everything is to be done in His name.

That's exactly what the apostle Paul said in Colossians 3:16–17. Notice these important verses, which give us the key to bringing all of life under the rule of Christ:

> Let the word of Christ dwell in you richly in all wisdom; teaching and admonishing one another in psalms and hymns and spiritual songs, singing with grace in your hearts to the Lord. And whatsoever ye do in word or deed, do all in the name of the Lord Jesus, giving thanks to God and the Father by him.

Look particularly at verse 17. "Whatsoever ye do" means everything, and therefore everything is to be done in the name of Jesus. That includes all of life. The scope of this exhortation is so wide that there's no room for the strictly secular. Even the so-called secular areas of life are to be sanctified, so that Jesus will be glorified in everything. Because He now lives in me, every day is a holy day, every time is a sacred time, and every task is a sacred task. The spiritual life is seven days a week.

What does it mean to do everything "in the name of the Lord Jesus"? One commentator says it means to live "in harmony with his revealed will, in subjection to his authority, in dependence on his power."[1] I think he has the idea. Jesus' revealed will is that which meets with His *approval*. Doing everything in His name certainly implies His *authority*. And when we act in dependence on Him, He wins the *acclaim* or glory.

Let's look at each of these in turn as we continue exploring what it means to be full-time temples of God.

The Approval of Jesus

In the Bible, as well as in life today, a man's name and his character are linked. So if we are to do everything in the name of Jesus, we must do only those things He can approve of.

One of the techniques that Madison Avenue uses in merchandising is to have a well-known personality endorse a product—that is, to lend his name and reputation to the product. This is frequently done by having the celebrity's picture or autograph inscribed upon some piece of merchandise. Many a little boy has wanted a specific baseball bat because his big-league hero had his name stamped on it.

That superstar was saying in effect, "I approve of this bat. It is consistent with the standards that I hold as a professional athlete, and it's just like the one I use."

In a similar way, to do everything in the name of Jesus means to do only that which He could endorse or approve. All that we do should be consistent with His character. We ought to do or say nothing that we could not sign Jesus' name to!

Rules Are for Kids

If *name* means character, then the character of Jesus, and not some set of rules, is the standard for our Christian lives. The Bible is not primarily a rule book with a list of dos and don'ts.

Rules are for kids. The more immature a child is, the more rules his parents must lay down for him. "Don't play with matches." "Come straight home from school." "Practice your music every day for forty-five minutes." The more mature child does not need rules like this. "The son who has come to years of responsibility knows his father's will without having to be provided with a long list of Do's and Don'ts."[2] The greater the maturity, the fewer the rules.

What a joy it was to me as a father when one of my children faced a situation about which we had not specifically talked and no rules had been laid down, and yet he came through with flying colors. "Daddy, I just did what I thought you would have wanted me to do. I knew you would approve." He did what he felt was consistent with my character.

This is a higher plane of living. One can find loopholes in rules. A lawyer reported to his client in a divorce case, "Mrs. Blake, I've succeeded in making a settlement with your husband that is eminently fair to both of you."

"Fair to both!" exploded Mrs. Blake. "I could have done that myself! What do you think I hired a lawyer for?"

One may twist the law, but he will never find a loophole in the character of Jesus. Therefore, the Bible is not primarily a book of minute laws but of great principles. And chief among them is to do all in the name of Jesus. We ought to be able to sign His name to our every action.

29

The Authority of Jesus

Not only does *name* stand for approval, but it also confers authority. The signature on a check gives the banker the authority to pay certain funds out of that account, as long as the check bears the name of a person who has money in that bank.

A policeman who weighs 140 pounds can stand before an 18-wheeler and with uplifted hand say, "Stop, in the name of the law." He is appealing to an authority higher than himself. The truck stops because of that name or authority. The policeman certainly did not, and could not, stop the truck with physical force. His badge and uniform carry the authority of the government he represents.

We need to learn a lesson right here. Our authority over Satan does not rest in the fact that we are stronger than he is. We indeed are not. Yet when Jesus sent out His disciples He said to them, "Behold, I give unto you power to tread on serpents and scorpions, and over all the power of the enemy: and nothing shall by any means hurt you" (Luke 10:19). What Jesus literally said was, "Behold, I have given you *authority* . . . over all the power of the enemy."

Note the difference between power and authority. The policeman stops the truck with authority, not with power. Likewise, we overcome Satan not with power, but with authority.

Knowing that *name* confers authority, we can understand more fully what it means to pray in the name of Jesus. To pray in His name does not necessarily mean that we close our prayers with the familiar formula, "In Jesus' name, Amen." I cannot find any prayer in the Bible that ends that way. I am not saying it's wrong to close a prayer in that manner, but that is not what Jesus meant when He taught us to pray in His name.

30

Spiritual Forgery

Prayer in Jesus' name is prayer that has His authority behind it. And remember, name means approval as well as authority. Therefore, I can guarantee you that no prayer will have Jesus' authority if it does not first of all have His approval. There are too many spiritual forgers signing Jesus' name to their prayer checks, but those checks will not be honored at the bank of heaven. There is no authority because there is no approval.

Are you living every day with the conscious authority of Christ in your life? You ought to do your housework, rear your children, earn your salary, and enjoy your leisure time with the authority of His mighty name. Every effort ought to be crowned with the power of heaven.

Let me say here that we can never have authority from Jesus to live as we ought until we are first of all submitted to Him. One of the greatest lessons I have ever learned is that I cannot be over until I'm willing to be under. I cannot have authority until I'm first of all submitted to authority.

We find an amazing example of this truth in Luke 7. A Roman army officer had a servant who was gravely ill. He sent some Jewish friends to ask Jesus to heal the servant, but as Jesus was coming to the house the centurion sent Him this message:

> Lord, trouble not thyself: for I am not worthy that thou shouldest enter under my roof: Wherefore neither thought I myself worthy to come unto thee: but say in a word, and my servant shall be healed. For I also am a man set under authority, having under me soldiers, and I say unto one, Go, and he goeth; and to another,

Come, and he cometh; and to my servant, Do this, and he doeth it. When Jesus heard these things, he marvelled at him, and turned him about, and said unto the people that followed him, I say unto you, I have not found so great faith, no, not in Israel. And they that were sent, returning to the house, found the servant whole that had been sick (vv. 6–10).

This man was a Gentile, but he had such an understanding of authority that Jesus marveled at him. He could command the soldiers under him, and they would go and come. This would continue to be true as long as he stayed under those who were over him. But should he step out from under this authority, he would lose the authority that was his to exercise over those under him.

The centurion then applied this principle to the work of Jesus. He said, in effect, "Jesus, because of Your submission to the Father over You, You have authority over this sickness. Just speak a word and my servant will be healed." The principle is clear—we cannot be over unless we are willing to be under.

What a tragedy when we live without the authority of God. There are pathetic preachers who preach without authority because they will not submit to the authority of the Word of God. They are the "bland leading the bland."

There are failing fathers who have no spiritual authority in the home because they have not submitted to the Lordship of Christ and to their elders in the church. Multitudes of mothers have no authority over their children because they will not submit to their own husbands as unto the Lord.

Think of the Christian young people who have no victory over the sins of the world, the flesh, and the devil because they are rebelling against their parents.

Many Christians, who ought to be victorious in their prayer life and have victory over the devil, are in a state of disarray because they are rebelling against the spiritual leadership that God has set up in the church.

Did you ever teach a youngster to drive a car? Suppose he says, "Dad, show me how to make it go! I've been wanting to get my hands on this baby for a long time."

You say, "Just a minute. Let me show you the brake first of all. You need to learn how to make it stop first."

"Oh, Dad," he replies, "I'm not interested in that. Show me how to make it go."

At that moment, the driving lesson is put on hold. So it is with the power of the Spirit. If we are not interested in the *restraint* of the Spirit, we have little hope of knowing the *release* of the Spirit. "In the name of Jesus" means with His authority because I am submitted to it.

The Acclaim of Jesus

Finally, doing everything in the name of Jesus means doing it for His acclaim or honor. Occasionally I receive a note telling me that a gift has been given to a certain cause in my name. That was the donor's way of saying that the gift was given in my honor or for my acclaim. I have learned to pass such honors on to Jesus because He's the only One Who is worthy of acclaim.

You see, as the temple of God, my life must be lived for only one purpose—that He will be glorified. This was Peter's goal. "If any man speak, let him speak as the oracles of God; if any man minister, let him do it as of the ability which God giveth: *that God in all things may be glorified through Jesus Christ*, to whom be praise and dominion for ever and ever. Amen" (1 Peter 4:11, italics added). Paul echoed the same desire: "Whether therefore ye eat, or drink, or whatsoever ye do, *do all to the glory of God*" (1 Corinthians 10:31, italics added).

As one who is indwelt by the Holy Spirit, you carry a tremendous responsibility to God and to man. If, indeed, the sign on your house says "Under New Management," you are *de facto* on display.

It is only the life that is lived with the approval of Jesus and in the authority of Jesus that will bring acclaim to Jesus. To live in the Spirit and to do everything in the name of Jesus means that we will do nothing to dishonor His name.

Just think what would happen if Christians started living this kind of a life every day and in every place. When God's people realize that they are to live what Oswald Chambers has called "naturally supernatural and supernaturally natural" lives, the world will begin to take notice. The best argument for Christianity, and sometimes the best argument *against* Christianity, is the life of a Christian. Not only are we to be His witnesses—we ought to be a part of the evidence!

CHAPTER THREE

Never Home Alone

A little girl was supposed to take her birth certificate to school. Her mother had solemnly warned her not to lose it because of its tremendous importance. But lose it she did. Later she was sitting on the steps of the schoolhouse, crying. The janitor asked her what was wrong. She replied, "I lost my excuse for being born."

Anybody who has not discovered the joy of salvation in Christ and the blessedness of being a temple of the Holy Spirit has indeed lost his excuse, his reason, for being born. Since salvation is the act by which the Spirit takes up His residence in us, we need to understand the importance and necessity of salvation and how man's house came to be empty. In the last chapter, we surveyed the house. Here we will look at the work of the Builder and Designer.

I like the word *saved*. Sophisticated theologians may want to steer away from that word because they think it sounds too common, language that belongs under the revival tent. But *saved* is a good word. Furthermore, it is a biblical word, just like its opposite, *lost*.

Saved and *lost* are important words because they describe two conditions of the human heart. They draw a clear line down the middle of the race. Everyone is either saved or lost. In the language of our analogy, whether you are saved or lost determines whether God dwells in your spiritual house or not. We know that no lost person can possibly be a temple of the Holy Spirit because a lost person does not possess the Spirit. "If any man have not the Spirit of Christ, he is none of his" (Romans 8:9).

I praise God that the Lord Jesus found me when I was a teenaged boy. I had never been in serious trouble, but I am sure I gave my parents a fair share of heartaches. My folks were good, hard-working, salt-of-the-earth kind of people. Dad earned his living in the automobile and furniture business. I had my share of whippings. Dad always said it was because he loved me. I have often thought that if that was so, I must have been his favorite child, for I received far more of this love than the rest of the kids!

But, like all of us, I needed something more in life than parental example and discipline. At an old-fashioned revival crusade in our hometown of West Palm Beach, Florida, my dad stepped out to give his heart and life to Christ. I followed right behind him. I believe that an eternal change took place in those moments, and that night I became a new creature in Christ. I was lost, but I got saved!

When God Moved Out

Before we can understand and appreciate fully what it means to be saved, we first have to understand what it means to be lost. The gospel has to be bad news before it can be good news.

Very simply, to be lost is to be in a state of spiritual death.

This spiritual death is best illustrated in the experience of Adam. His death and our deaths are linked. "In Adam all die"

(1 Corinthians 15:22). But if we died in Adam, just how did Adam die?

You will recall that God had placed Adam and Eve in the Garden of Eden, where He had given them all that they needed to be healthy, happy, and holy. He had made ample provision for Adam—body, soul, and spirit. At that time, God Himself lived as a Royal Resident in His first temple, named Adam.

But in order for man to have the ability to truly love God, he had to have the opportunity to choose not to love God. A choice had to be given. God described the basis of that choice to Adam:

> And the LORD God took the man, and put him into the garden of Eden to dress it and to keep it. And the LORD God commanded the man, saying, Of every tree of the garden thou mayest freely eat: But of the tree of the knowledge of good and evil, thou shalt not eat of it: for in the day that thou eatest thereof thou shalt surely die (Genesis 2:15–17).

When God spoke of death, He was not giving a threat but a warning. Parents are not threatening their children when they warn them about a hot stove. If Adam chose not to love God enough to obey Him, he would die.

What is the record? What did Adam do? "When the woman saw that the tree was good for food, and that it was pleasant to the eyes, and a tree to be desired to make one wise, she took of the fruit thereof, and did eat, and gave also unto her husband with her; and he did eat" (Genesis 3:6).

When Adam disobeyed God, he insulted his Royal Guest. He didn't commit murder or adultery, but he failed to love and obey God. This was his great sin. Adam was no longer a clean and holy house. He was now defiled by sin.

The sure and swift result of Adam's sin was death. We just read it. God had said, "In the day that thou eateth thereof thou shalt surely die" (Genesis 2:17). But wait a minute! Did Adam "surely die"? The Bible records that he went on to live for many hundreds of years! There has been endless discussion and controversy about how, and even if, Adam died on the day he sinned. Indeed he died, but it is so important to understand just how he died.

First, Adam died *immediately* in his spirit. Death in the biblical sense is not primarily the separation of the soul from the body, as we think of death. For example, if I were to drop this pen and get very still and stay that way for a long time, some doctor might take my vital signs and say, "He is dead."

But biblically speaking that would be inaccurate. I would simply have moved out of this earthly "house" and gone on to heaven. Jesus said, "Whosoever liveth and believeth in me shall never die" (John 11:26). So how could I be dead? I would be more alive than ever. And while you attended my funeral, I would be "kicking up gold-dust on the streets of Glory," as one writer has put it. For "to be absent from the body [is] to be present with the Lord" (2 Corinthians 5:8).

What I am saying is that spiritual death is far different than physical death. Spiritual death is not the separation of the soul from the body, but the separation of the spirit from God. Adam died spiritually that very day, even though he was left standing on his feet. What happened was that God's Holy Spirit moved out. God will not live in a dirty house. Adam came under what the Scripture calls the condemnation of sin and death.

A group of college boys wanted to keep the football team mascot—a goat—so they made intricate plans to smuggle the animal into their dormitory room.

"But what about the smell?" someone asked.

"The goat will just have to get used to it," the others replied.

College boys may be content to live in a dirty place, but a holy God will not do so. It is against His very nature.

What was the result of God's moving out of Adam? God's Spirit is to the human spirit as blood is to the body. He is the life-giving power of the human spirit. John said, "In him was life; and the life was the light of men" (John 1:4). These words are speaking of Christ, but what is true of Christ is true of the Spirit as well. God is the light and the life of man.

So when Adam sinned, *the Lord went out.* And when the Lord went out, *the life went out.* And when the life went out, *the light went out.* Adam was now spiritually depraved—no Lord. He was spiritually dead—no life. He was spiritually darkened—no light. It was not until centuries later that the death, burial, and resurrection of Jesus Christ would deal with all three of these problems.

Adam not only died immediately in his spirit, but he died *progressively* in his soul. His spirit was supposed to receive directions from God's Spirit. "For as many as are led by the Spirit of God, they are the sons of God" (Romans 8:14). Adam's spirit was, in turn, to give directions to his soul (mind, emotions, and will), which would then motivate and direct his body.

Man was not given the sense of instinct that most animals have. The reason for this is that God made His Holy Spirit available to man. In one sense, the Spirit should be to man what instinct is to the other creatures. Can you imagine the confusion if instinct were removed from bees? Or from birds as they prepare to head south? Or from a guard dog as he senses danger? Take a look at what we call "civilization" and you will have some idea of the result when God's Spirit moved out of man!

So Adam was minus God in his spirit. God no longer lived in him and walked with him. Adam was no longer a *spiritual* man. He was now a *natural* man. That is, sin had reduced him to operating by his soul alone. His spiritual transmitter was jammed. His *mind* became a garden of weeds. His *emotions* began to churn with fear. His *will* was corrupt and paralyzed. He was free to do what he wanted, but not free to do as he ought.

Rather than becoming the master over his house, Adam became the household slave when he rebelled against God. When God moved out, Adam's soul (mind, emotions, and will) took over the control center. Now Adam would operate not as a God-centered man, but as a self-centered man, dominated by sin.

Ever notice how a natural man operates? His mind says, "I think I want to do thus-and-so." His emotions say, "I feel like doing it." His will says, "All right, I'll do it."

Do you know anybody who lives like that? The world is filled with such people. They are the living dead! It sounds like a horror movie, doesn't it? Well, it is horrible, but sadly it's not a movie! All you have to do is watch the evening news to realize that we are living in a chamber of horrors where everyone does exactly whatever he pleases.

Even Christians operate this way all too often. But what does the Bible say? "She that liveth in pleasure is dead while she liveth" (1 Timothy 5:6).

Adam died immediately in his spirit and progressively in his soul. He also died *ultimately* in his body. "And all the days that Adam lived were nine hundred and thirty years: and he died" (Genesis 5:5).

Now, at last, his body had ceased to function. Adam, however, had been dead long before this. He was like a Christmas tree, cut off from the root (the transmitter of life) and brought into your living room. It looks good in your house with all of its colorful ornaments and lights. That is, it looks good until about New Year's Day! By then, what happened to the tree when it was cut off has gradually become obvious by outward signs of deadness.

Similarly, many people who are severed from God through sin decorate themselves and even come to church on Sunday morning and try to worship. They may look very good, but there's no life there. They may even try to please God, but they cannot pull it off. Their temples are adorned but empty. Their houses are brightly decorated, but there's no one home.

Many are aware that something is wrong, and they are miserable. They are cut off from the Source of true life and are dead spiritually. Ultimately they will die physically as well. It has been well said that the heartbeat in your chest is but "a muffled drum beating a funeral march to the grave."

So God's first temple was Adam, but God moved out of Adam. And when God moved out, Adam died. And Adam's death has been passed on to each of us. "Wherefore, as by one man sin entered into the world, and death by sin; and so death passed upon all men, for that all have sinned" (Romans 5:12). The Bible teaches that we all died in Adam, the result of what theologians call "original sin."

When God Moves Back In

But now comes the good part. Salvation is not merely about getting man out of earth into heaven. It is also about getting God out of heaven and back into man! Here's something exciting: when a person receives Christ and is born again, God reverses the effects of sin!

Adam died immediately in his spirit, progressively in his soul, and ultimately in his body. But when one becomes a child of God, he is *justified immediately in his spirit, sanctified progressively in his soul, and glorified ultimately in his body!*

Nearly two thousand years ago, God the Father made His final move to gain back His dwelling-place among men. By the work of His Holy Spirit in the womb of a godly peasant woman named Mary, the eternal Son of God—the Second Person of the Trinity—assumed human flesh, became man, and was born on earth.

Jesus Christ, from that miracle on, was and is fully God and fully man. They called His name Immanuel—"God with us!" As the firstborn of a whole new race, those with whom God dwells, Jesus proved to us that God could inhabit humanity.

But this was not all. God's justice demands that our sin be dealt with. Jesus died to remove the sin barrier so that God can once more dwell in man. It was sin that caused God to move out, and He cannot return until that sin is properly dealt with. This is why the cross was necessary.

If we were to choose one word to describe the character of God, it might be love because "God is love" (1 John 4:8). In fact, He is perfect love. But let me suggest a word that perhaps best epitomizes the character of God: *holy*. He is the thrice-holy God, for Isaiah tells us, "Holy, holy, holy, is the LORD of hosts" (Isaiah 6:3).

God's holiness demands that sin be properly judged. If God were to merely overlook our sin, He would cease to be holy. In a court of law, it is said that when a guilty man is acquitted, the judge is condemned. God "will not at all acquit the wicked" (Nahum 1:3).

But through faith in Christ's finished work at Calvary, we who believe are immediately justified in the spirit:

Now to him that worketh is the reward not reckoned of grace, but of debt. But to him that worketh not, but believeth on him that justifieth the ungodly, his faith is counted for righteousness. Even as David also describeth the blessedness of the man, unto whom God imputeth righteousness without works, saying, Blessed are they whose iniquities are forgiven, and whose sins are covered. Blessed is the man to whom the Lord will not impute sin (Romans 4:4–8).

God is now free to move into the cleansed temple of our bodies and to dwell in us because the barrier of sin has been taken away.

But not only are we justified immediately in the spirit—we can also be sanctified progressively in the soul. Our minds, emotions, and wills can be taken captive by the Holy Spirit within the human spirit, and we can begin to live like the people we have become.

Remember that while justification is immediate, sanctification is a process that will not be finished until we are with Jesus. "Being confident of this very thing, that he which hath begun a good work in you will perform it until the day of Jesus Christ" (Philippians 1:6).

After my salvation, I discovered that old habits and ways die hard. The cheating in class, the school-yard fights, truancy, bad language, and disobedience still pulled at me. I was up and down in my Christian life for over a year, and I was miserable.

One night after I had walked my girlfriend home from church, I stopped and prayed. I was tired of the struggle, the doubt, the failure. Also, I had by this time learned more of the truth of God. "Lord Jesus," I prayed, "right now, with all of my heart, once and for all, now and forever, I trust You and You alone to save me according to the promise of Your Word. If I have never really trusted You, I do so now. If I am already saved, then I reaffirm it. But one thing I know is that I am driving down a spiritual peg tonight. I do not ask for feeling. I stand upon Your promise, Lord Jesus, and I know that settles it!"

At that moment, a wonderful river of God's peace and assurance began to flow through my heart. And, praise His name, it has never stopped flowing.

As a young man I had thought seriously about being a lawyer or an architect. But now I knew that God had a right to make these choices in my life. He would lead me into His will, and He would decide for the best. "Lord, whatever You want me to do, I'll do it. Just let me know," I prayed.

I am not sure exactly how the seed-thought that God might want me to preach got into my heart. But I found it there. "Lord, do You really want me to preach?" I would ask Him. As a high-school football player, I was not afraid of much that moved on the gridiron, but the thought of being a public speaker was disturbing. More candidly, it scared me to death.

Yet, this little seed of a thought would not go away. For weeks I would pray like this: "Lord, I think You want me to preach." Then for days I would pray, "Lord, if You don't want me to preach, You had better let me know." Finally it was, "Lord, You are calling me, and I know it."

I finally made a public commitment, and it was settled. From that point on I did not look back. I was thrilled that God would call me to serve Him in this way. Joyce, my high-school sweetheart who became my wife, was also thrilled. In her heart, she sensed God calling her into His full-time service as well. This was all a part of the process of sanctification in our lives.

But someday the process will be complete. Ultimately, we will also be glorified in our bodies. Every Christian should be looking for the coming of the Lord Jesus, "who shall change our vile body, that it may be fashioned like unto his glorious body, according to the working whereby he is able even to subdue all things under himself" (Philippians 3:21).

Therefore, it is not until we receive our glorified bodies at the resurrection that our salvation will be complete. It unfolds in three stages:

Past tense: I have been justified in my spirit and have been saved from the penalty of sin.

Present tense: I am being sanctified in my soul and am being saved from the power of sin.

Future tense: I will be glorified in my body and will be saved from the possibility of sin.

But until the time of my glorification, I have a Royal Resident who lives within me and has promised He will never leave or forsake me (Hebrews 13:5). Is anybody home in your house today?

CHAPTER FOUR

When Glory Fills the House

When King Solomon dedicated that magnificent temple on Mount Moriah it was, among other things, an object lesson, an illustration of every believer in the Lord Jesus Christ. For now, after Pentecost, at the moment of our salvation, we become temples of the Holy Spirit. God through His Holy Spirit indwells us, just as His Spirit came and filled the holy of holies of Solomon's temple with shekinah glory when it was fully dedicated to Him: "And it came to pass, when the priests were come out of the holy place, that the cloud filled the house of the LORD, so that the priests could not stand to minister because of the cloud: for the glory of the LORD had filled the house of the LORD" (1 Kings 8:10–11).

Yet, some Christians appear not to be filled with the Holy Spirit. Glory does not fill their house. They have allowed the self-life and the cares of this world to move the Lord Jesus from that place of preeminence that is rightfully His. They are no longer Spirit-filled but are what the Bible calls "carnal" or fleshly. Therefore, we have this admonition of the apostle Paul: "Be not drunk with wine, wherein is excess; but be filled with the Spirit" (Ephesians 5:18).

In this chapter, I want to address this matter of the Spirit-filled life. I need to emphasize here that a Spirit-filled Christian is not some super-edition of a Christian. He is not a regular believer raised to the highest power! When the God of the universe moves into our lives, He won't be relegated to a back room. He wants to fill the whole house!

Thus *all* Christians ought to be experiencing the Spirit-filled life. It is the normal Christian life. The fullness of the Spirit is not some special touch for the evangelist or minister but is a provision for every blood-bought child of God. "The promise is unto you, and to your children, and to all that are afar off, even as many as the LORD our God shall call" (Acts 2:39).

Since all of this is true, we had better find out what's involved in letting God the Holy Spirit fill every corner of our houses. In Ephesians 5 and 6, Paul gave the reasons, the requirements, and the results of the Spirit-filled life.

Reasons for the Spirit-filled Life

I see at least three reasons why Christians need to live Spirit-filled lives.

OBEDIENCE

The first reason for any Christian to be Spirit-filled is simple obedience. God has told us, "Be filled with the Spirit" (Ephesians 5:18). This is not a suggestion or a request but a command. The Christian who is not Spirit-filled is actually living in rebellion. His disobedience to God is not weakness but wickedness.

Any congregation would be scandalized should the minister attempt to preach a sermon while drunk. His thick tongue, bleary eyes, and foolish thoughts would cause a quick meeting of the elders, deacons, or other official bodies within the church. What a disgraceful thing it would be. How tongues would wag!

Yet, I sincerely believe it would be a greater sin for any man of God to fail to be filled with the Spirit when preaching than to be drunk. The same verse that commands us not to be "drunk with wine" commands us to be "filled with the Spirit."

The Scripture also teaches that sins of omission are just as offensive to God as sins of commission (James 4:17). In a sense, it is a greater sin to fail to do what we ought than to do what we ought not. As a matter of fact, if we are doing what we ought to do, we cannot be doing what we ought not to do.

Now, I am not minimizing the sin of drunkenness or any other sin. But in my estimation, the cause of Christ has been hurt far more by Christians who are carnal and not Spirit-filled than by Christians who are drunk. I have known of churches torn apart by carnal leadership. Many people who are at the forefront of church splits are teetotalers. The devil would rather start a fuss in the Body of Christ than sell a barrel of whiskey any day.

It is important for us to understand that the Spirit-filled life is not an option. It is not merely a blessing to enjoy; it is a command to obey. To fail to obey is a sin worse than being drunk.

OBLIGATION

A second reason Paul gave for being filled with the Spirit is that it is our obligation. As Christians, we have tremendous responsibilities to fulfill.

Look at the obligation of our *worship life*. "Speaking to yourselves in psalms and hymns and spiritual songs, singing and making melody in your heart to the Lord" (Ephesians

5:19). Our worship life is to be alive with joy and the reality of Christ. This kind of worship is the overflow of the Spirit-filled life. It is what Jesus called "worship him in spirit" (John 4:24).

Yet, many Christians would confess that for them, worship could be more aptly described by the words of the hymn, "How Tedious and Tasteless the Hours."

Look at the obligation of our *wedded life*. "Wives, submit yourselves unto your own husbands, as unto the Lord" (Ephesians 5:22). In this day of radical feminism, the role of the submitted wife is doubly difficult. Many, even in the church, teach that verses like this are simply tools of a male-dominated establishment that seeks to oppress women. To put it mildly, submission is not popular. But the fact of the matter is, this has never been done in any age apart from the power of the Holy Spirit.

Further, submission does not mean the woman is inferior. Everyone knows that a woman is infinitely superior to a man—at being a woman! And the man is infinitely superior to a woman—at being a man! God made us different so He could make us one.

It is Satan's lie that submission means inferiority. I like to think of what happened in the Garden of Eden as a three-act tragedy: Adam's rib, Satan's fib, and a wrong sort of women's lib. A woman is truly liberated by the Spirit of God when she is freed not only to do what she wants, but to do what she ought. And God says she will find her freedom in obeying her husband.

Paul's command is not one-sided. "Husbands, love your wives, even as Christ also loved the church, and gave himself for it" (Ephesians 5:25). How does Jesus love the church? He loves it sacrificially and completely. A husband should be willing to die for his wife, but he need not die physically in order to live sacrificially for her.

Note that far more is required of the husband than of the wife. The wife's model is the church, but the husband's is Christ Himself. How is any mortal man going to do anything as Jesus does it? There is no way apart from the Spirit-filled life. I am encouraged by the emerging movement in the Body of Christ to call men to faithfulness as husbands and fathers.

Look at the obligation of our *work life*. "Servants, be obedient to them that are your masters according to the flesh, with fear and trembling, in singleness of your heart, as unto Christ; not with eyeservice, as menpleasers; but as the servants of Christ, doing the will of God from the heart" (Ephesians 6:5–6). Work for our employers as though they were the Lord Jesus Christ? That's what Paul said!

When an employer calls an employment agency looking for new workers, he ought to say (if Christians were generally what they are meant to be in this area), "If you have any Christians, please give them the first opportunity. I don't understand it, but they are different from my other workers. They are on time; they do not gossip, cheat, or steal. They work hard. You would think that they think I am the Lord." I am convinced that if more employees began to live like that on Monday, far more employers would believe what is preached on Sunday.

Look at the obligation of our *war life*. "For we wrestle not against flesh and blood, but against principalities, against powers, against the rulers of the darkness of this world, against spiritual wickedness in high places" (Ephesians 6:12). The Christian is at war! Ours is a fight to the finish with a sinister foe, and there are no holds barred. Satan is our adversary who has let loose with all the artillery of hell.

We will never defeat him with the weak efforts of our human flesh. If the battle were against mere humanity, then flesh might defeat flesh. But this is a spiritual war. Satan laughs at our organizations and mocks our schemes, but he trembles before the mighty power of God released through a Spirit-filled saint. I pity the Christian soldier who fights Satan with his own puny human strength.

OPPORTUNITIES

A third reason for being filled with the Spirit is our opportunities. "Redeeming the time, because the days are evil. Wherefore be ye not unwise, but understanding what the will of the Lord is" (Ephesians 5:16–17). These verses come just before the command to be filled with the Spirit. It is God's reminder that we are to use our time and opportunities wisely.

Any day that is not crowned with the Christian being consciously and conspicuously filled with the Holy Spirit is a wasted day. It will be lost for all eternity. At the judgment seat of Christ it will, at best, be counted as wood, hay, and stubble (1 Corinthians 3:12).

What golden opportunities we let slip through our fingers because the Spirit is not in control. There has never been a greater day or age to witness for Christ than ours. There is such a need and such a hunger everywhere.

But I have noticed a subtle yet deadly thing happening in the lives of some Christians. They see the Spirit-filled life simply as a source of enjoyment rather than a force of employment. They are interested in spiritual gifts—but as toys rather than tools. Consider, for example, the "health and wealth" gospel that is preached so fervently today by what I call the "happiness boys."

A woman was giving a word of appreciation to her first-aid class. She said, "There was a terrible accident in front of my house. A man was lying there with bones splintered, rolling around in pools of blood. His arteries were severed. He was in a state of shock. But I remembered my first-aid instructions that if I would put my head between my knees, I wouldn't faint. It worked, and I didn't faint. I am so grateful that I took this class."

Some Christians are like that. We need to get our heads from between our knees and realize that Jesus said, "Ye shall receive power, after that the Holy Ghost is come upon you: and ye shall be witnesses unto me both in Jerusalem, and in all Judaea, and in Samaria, and unto the uttermost part of the earth" (Acts 1:8).

We are filled with the Holy Spirit in order to "Rescue the perishing / Care for the dying / Tell them of Jesus, the mighty to save."[1] Our opportunities give us good reason to be Spirit-filled.

Requirements for the Spirit-filled Life

How does the Holy Spirit fill us? In answering this question, it should be noted that the Holy Spirit is a Person, just as God the Father and God the Son are Persons. The Spirit acts, wills, and loves, and He may be grieved or insulted. I say this because some people think of the Holy Spirit merely as some kind of impersonal force or power emanating from God.

The Holy Spirit does indeed have force and power, but He is a Person. So the concept of being filled with the Holy Spirit is not that of a vessel being filled by some substance or a machine being supercharged with power, but of a human house being completely occupied by a divine Person. We are not co-mingled with God. We are still human, and He is forever divine. But we are empowered by Him, used by Him.

With that concept in mind, let us consider three requirements for the Spirit-filled life.

TOTAL COMMITMENT

First, there must be a *complete commitment to the Spirit*. All of us have had guests in our homes. We double up the kids in one room and make a place for the newcomers. We clear a space in the closet for their clothes. "Here's your room," we tell them. "Here's the bath. Here are the extra towels. Here's the refrigerator and a key to the house. Make yourself at home. Our house is your house," we say.

But suppose you come home one day to find your guest in your own bedroom going through your personal records. He is reading your old love letters, your tax reports, and your will. You clear your throat and try to be calm as you ask, "Are you looking for something I can help you with?" But by the tone of your voice you are really asking, "What are you doing in here? You have no business in my personal papers!"

Your guest replies, "No, thank you. I don't need any help. I was just curious about your personal affairs and thought these things would be interesting reading."

By this time, you cannot control your anger. "You have no business prying into my personal papers. That desk should not concern you. Please close it immediately."

Your guest responds, "I don't understand you. You said that I was to make myself at home, that your house was my house."

"Well, I didn't mean that you are free to pry into my personal affairs." And a friendship begins to unravel.

Have you ever been guilty of doing something like that to the Holy Spirit? "Dear Holy Spirit, come and live in the temple of my body. My heart is Your abode. Make Yourself completely at home." But the searching question is, have you given Him the key to every room, every closet, every desk? Is there any part of your life that is off-limits to your heavenly Guest?

If so, you are not filled with the Spirit. Remember, we said it is impossible for the great God of the universe to be relegated to a back room of His own temple.

The Holy Spirit must have the key to your business life, your social life, your thought life, *everything*. The Holy Spirit deserves and demands access to every corner of the temple that Christ purchased with His blood. "What? know ye not that your body is the temple of the Holy Ghost which is in you, which ye have of God, and ye are not your own?" (1 Corinthians 6:19). He will not settle for one room—even a prominent one. He demands preeminence.

In the last century, some ministers were planning a united crusade. They met to select an evangelist. The majority wanted Dwight L. Moody, the great preacher who was filled with the Spirit and anointed with God's mighty power, to preach His Word.

One minister on the committee, however, was holding out for another evangelist. In exasperation he finally said, "Moody, Moody, Moody . . . That is the only name you seem to know. Does Moody have a monopoly on the Holy Spirit?"

One of the others answered, "No, but it seems that the Holy Spirit has a monopoly on Moody."

Moody himself said, "I know perfectly well that, wherever I go to preach, there are many better preachers known and heard than I am; all that I can say about it is that the Lord uses me."[2]

That's what I'm talking about. Does the Holy Spirit have a monopoly on you? Have you given Him the key to every room? Is He merely a resident, or is He president? Have you made a complete commitment to Him?

TOTAL POSSESSION

The second requirement for the Spirit-filled life is *continual control by the Spirit.* Ephesians 5:18 may be translated, "Be ye being filled with the Spirit." This matter of the Spirit-filled life is not a once-for-all matter. To be sure, there may be a crisis experience when we yield our all to Him, but this crisis is followed by a process. The Holy Spirit's control must be recognized day by day as we yield to Him.

We saw that the command is, "Be not drunk with wine . . . but be filled with the Spirit." Why didn't the Lord say, "Don't commit adultery, but be filled with the Spirit"? Or why didn't He name lying, stealing, pride, or some other sin in contrast to being Spirit-filled?

The answer is that He was speaking both by way of contrast and comparison. There is a sense in which the result of being Spirit-filled may be compared to being intoxicated. The disciples were accused of being drunk with new wine when they were filled with the Spirit on the Day of Pentecost. But Peter answered, "These are not drunken, as ye suppose" (Acts 2:15). The people who were watching the disciples automatically assumed that no one would act like that unless he was drunk.

When a man is drunk, he is brought under the control of another power. Liquor has been called "the devil in liquid form." Satan uses it to take over a man's life. His walk, his talk, his thoughts, his courage, and his morals all change for the worse. But when a man is Spirit-filled, they are changed for the better.

Here is the point. How does a man get drunk? By drinking! But how does he stay drunk? He must keep on drinking. I believe I know some Christians who were once Spirit-filled, but they've "sobered up." As Christians, we must keep drinking from that fountain that never shall run dry.

In order for there to be continual control, there must be continual appropriation of the dear Holy Spirit in all of His fullness. Remember that He is a Person and not a substance like wine. But as a drunkard yields totally to alcohol and is thoroughly affected by it, so as we yield to the Spirit totally He affects our whole personality.

DELIBERATE ACCEPTANCE

The third requirement of the Spirit-filled life is that of a *conscious claiming of the Spirit*. Remember that when the Holy Spirit came to live within you, He came in as a divine Person. It is so easy to miss what Paul is saying. He does not say to be filled *by* the Spirit but *with* the Spirit. We must not get the idea that the Holy Spirit is waiting outside of us to place into us what we need.

If that were so, we might say, "I need more love," and He would fill us with love. Or, "I need more patience," and He would pour in the patience. But that is not the idea at all. That would be being filled by the Spirit. We are to be filled with the Spirit Himself. He floods every area of our lives with His blessed self.

Therefore, when He is present in our lives, we have all the love, patience, or anything else that we could ever need. In Him we are complete.

A country pastor's wife was at her wit's end. She was left alone with two active children while her husband commuted to the seminary for his weekday studies. The pressures upon her were terrific, and she cried out to God for help. "Give me more patience, Lord. Give me more strength. Give me more love." Yet she had no victory.

One day it dawned upon her that through the Holy Spirit, Jesus was alive and well and living within the temple of her body. Her prayers began to change. She no longer prayed, "Give me more patience, Lord." Now her prayer was, "Thy patience, Lord."

She made a conscious claiming of that which was already hers. All that she needed, she already had. She recognized the presence and gracious sufficiency of the Holy Spirit in her. The supply of her every need was just waiting to be claimed by faith.

Immediately there was a new release of power in her life as God's Holy Spirit expressed His love, patience, and strength through her. The difference was dramatic.

Results of the Spirit-filled Life

The verses that follow the command to be filled with the Spirit in Ephesians 5 speak of the results that are sure to manifest themselves when the Lord Jesus Christ is enthroned in the holy temple of our bodies, when His glory fills our house. All of us live in relationship to God, circumstances, and others. The Spirit-filled life affects each of these.

AN ATTITUDE OF WORSHIP

In our relationship to God, there will be a *spirit of adoration*. We quoted Ephesians 5:19 earlier in this chapter. As we have already noted, it is the holy obligation and blessed privilege of the people of God to worship the Lord in the Spirit.

As our means of adoration, Paul spoke of "psalms and hymns and spiritual songs." The Old Testament "psalms" were the songbook both of Israel and of the early church. "Hymns" and songs of praise issue forth adoration directly to God.

"Spiritual songs" seem to mean joyful and spontaneous music that overflows from the heart.

The whole idea is that Spirit-filled worship, whether congregational or personal, is to come joyfully from the heart and is to be unto the Lord.

It seems almost a truism to say that songs of worship should be sung "to the Lord." Yet this definitely needs to be said. Much of the music in our churches today is not real worship at all but is merely flesh on parade. Just as we may pray to be "seen of men" (Matthew 6:5), we can sing the same way. We are often singing one to another rather than to the Lord.

Perhaps the worst thing that could be said about some music is not that it is off-key, but rather that it is sung to the wrong audience. I have observed that when music is truly sung to the Lord, it speaks to the congregation also.

I am also convinced that God is not all that impressed with musical perfection. None of us should ever do less than his best musically, but for some of us our best is not so great. One minister of music called me a "prisoner-singer." He said, "You are always behind a few bars and can't find the right key."

Be that as it may, God would just as soon hear a blackbird sing as a nightingale, and I am convinced that He is pleased when I make melody in my heart. Actually, the phrase "making melody" means to strum an instrument. Therefore, I am to make music not *in* my heart, but *with* my heart. My heart is to be the instrument of praise for God's glory.

AN ATTITUDE OF THANKSGIVING

In our relationship to circumstances, the result of the Spirit-filled life will be a *spirit of appreciation*—"giving thanks always for all things unto God and the Father in the name of our Lord Jesus Christ" (Ephesians 5:20).

Perhaps the most common but often-transgressed command in the Bible is the command to be thankful. A carnal Christian is often grumbly hateful. The Spirit-filled Christian is humbly grateful.

This command to be thankful would not be such a difficult one had the Lord not said "always" and "all things."

> *We thank Him for sun,*
> *Do we thank Him for rain?*
> *We thank Him for joy,*
> *Do we thank Him for pain?*
> *We thank Him for gains,*
> *Do we thank Him for losses?*
> *We thank Him for blessings,*
> *Do we thank Him for crosses?*

To give thanks when there is personal hurt, cancer, divorce, financial reverse, or heartbreaking disappointment seems to be unnatural. But when we give thanks, we are not necessarily expressing approval of those things for which we give thanks. We are rather announcing our confidence that our God is greater than any of these things.

Allow me to give you a very personal and painful example of a time when I learned this truth firsthand. After our seminary days, Joyce and I were called back to Florida to a fine little church in Fort Pierce. By this time we had three children— Stephen, Gayle, and Phillip. Phillip was only two months old when we got settled in the new parsonage, nestled right next door to the little white cement-block church.

It happened on a beautiful Mother's Day. I had just preached a Mother's Day message on the blessings of a Christian home. Joyce was out in the kitchen of our small house preparing lunch after the service. I was in the living room reading.

Suddenly, I heard her distraught voice. "Adrian," she cried, "come here quickly! Something is wrong with Phillip!"

I leaped to my feet. She had our baby boy in her arms. He was not breathing. His face had a blue cast upon it.

"What's wrong?" she cried.

"I don't know. You call the hospital and tell them I'm coming."

I took our little boy and put him inside my coat to keep him warm. With eyes blinded by tears, I screeched out of our driveway and sped to the emergency room. "Please help me!" I cried to a waiting nurse as I burst through the heavy double doors to the hospital. Kind hands took Phillip and rushed him into a nearby room. I kneeled outside that emergency-room door and prayed for God's mercy, not caring who saw me or what they might think.

After a while, an attending doctor came out of the room, without Phillip, and walked over to me. "He's gone," he said as he laid his hand on my shoulder and shook his head. "There was nothing we could do. We tried."

It was one of those sudden "crib deaths."

Joyce was standing in the doorway of our house when I returned alone. The look on my face told the story. Mother's Day had turned into a day of incredible grief and confusion for us. We had not known death in either of our families. It was so sudden, so stark. We did the only thing we knew to do. We kneeled and called out to the Lord for help.

Then we turned to the Word of God. I wasn't sure where to begin reading. But the Lord led us to the message we so sorely needed. This is what God said:

> Grace be to you and peace from God our Father, and from the Lord Jesus Christ. Blessed be God, even the Father of our Lord Jesus Christ, the Father of mercies, and the God of all comfort;

who comforteth us in all our tribulation, that we may be able to comfort them which are in any trouble, by the comfort wherewith we ourselves are comforted of God (2 Corinthians 1:2–4).

I did not understand all that God was allowing to happen to us. But He had already made one thing abundantly clear: the Father of mercies was going to use our sorrow to help us be a blessing to other broken hearts. We gave our brokenness and confusion to the God of all comfort.

That Sunday afternoon we drove to our parents' homes. The church had gotten someone to fill the pulpit for me for the evening service. The services were just beginning as we backed out of the driveway. I can still hear the congregation today as they were singing, "No, never alone / no, never alone / He promised never to leave me / Never to leave me alone."[3]

Joyce and I willed to worship the Lord together, and we sang every praise song we knew as we drove those sixty miles back to our hometown. And it was so very true. *We were not alone!* God's presence was never more real.

In the days and months that followed, we sought the Lord in a new way. Then, by God's grace, a friend and fellow pastor came to our church and preached a message on the Spirit-filled life. Our hungry hearts reached up and received the truth, and the transformation took place. The Lord Jesus truly was alive in us and was just waiting to take over.

You see, since God is love and God is sovereign, there is no area where He does not lovingly rule or overrule—even in tragedy. Nothing comes to us unless He allows it. Not a blade of grass moves without His permission. Romans 8:28 is always true: "And we know that all things work together for good to them that love God, to them who are the called according to his purpose." Therefore, we can give thanks.

AN ATTITUDE OF ACCOMMODATION

In our relationship to others, a Spirit-filled life will result in a *spirit of accommodation*: "Submitting yourselves one to another in the fear of God" (Ephesians 5:21).

When a person consistently insists on standing up for his rights, he may know little of the Spirit-filled life. We have been crucified with Christ. What rights does a dead man have? What did Paul say about our rights? "Ye are not your own"!

In earthly relationships, submission is one equal willingly and lovingly placing himself or herself under another equal so that Jesus will be glorified. "We preach not ourselves, but Christ Jesus the Lord; and ourselves your servants for Jesus' sake" (2 Corinthians 4:5).

We do not submit to one another because of one another as such, but because of the Lord Jesus Christ. Submission, therefore, is not only for wives. It is for Christians!

The Spirit-filled life is for all of us who know Jesus Christ. Why settle for anything less than God's best for you? Why invite the Spirit of God to take up residence in your house and then try to shut Him up in the closet?

Remember, it is not your job to persuade Him to fill you but to *permit* Him to do so when you give Him the key to every room in your house. You do not need anything more and should never be content with anything less.

CHAPTER FIVE

Supernatural or Superficial?

A noted Southern Baptist preacher, the late Dr. Robert G. Lee, once preached an excoriating sermon against sin. He didn't pull any punches. A lady whose feathers had been ruffled met him at the door and said, "I didn't appreciate that sermon one little bit."

Dr. Lee reportedly replied, "The devil didn't either. So classify yourself."

Classification is not always flattering, but it is always needed in spiritual matters. The Bible teaches that in the broad sense there are three categories or classes of people living on Planet Earth. In 1 Corinthians 2–3 the apostle Paul called them the natural man, the spiritual man, and the carnal man. For our purposes, we might also think of them as three kinds of houses or dwellings.

Classification is important because it is the starting point in our understanding of the life of faith. Just as no one really grasps his need to be saved until he realizes he is lost, so we cannot get to where we ought to be in our spiritual pilgrimage until we recognize where we are.

We need to know into which of Paul's three classifications we fit. Armed with this insight, we can then lay a proper spiritual foundation as we build a home for Christ in our hearts. As we study the characteristics of the natural man, the spiritual man, and the carnal man, may God show us where our house is out of line with His blueprint and help set our spiritual house in order.

Doing What Comes Naturally

Let's look at these categories in 1 Corinthians 2–3. Meet first the natural man. Here's how he looks to God: "The natural man receiveth not the things of the Spirit of God: for they are foolishness unto him: neither can he know them, because they are spiritually discerned" (2:14).

Why do we call the natural man by such a term? Because he is just that—natural. He is the sum total of all that he has received by nature from his first birth . . . and nothing more.

He is born into the natural world. He may have been born well physically, receiving many admirable traits through his natural birth. He may be witty, charming, cultured, outwardly moral, and educated. Why, he may even be religious! But because the natural man has had no second birth, he is dead to the spiritual world. Having been born only once, he is spiritually dead. Naturally!

How do we know the natural man is spiritually dead? Because as we saw earlier, the Scripture says, "In Adam all die" (1 Corinthians 15:22). What does that mean? Let us do a quick review.

Remember that Adam was designed to be a house inhabited by the Lord. God's Holy Spirit was to indwell and give life to Adam's human spirit. But when Adam sinned, he died. He did not die an immediate physical death, but he did die spiritually at that moment. We said that spiritual death is the separation of the Spirit of God from the spirit of man. God moved out of Adam's spirit; Adam became devoid of God in his spirit.

Concerning our Lord Jesus, God says by way of contrast, "In him was life; and the life was the light of men" (John 1:4). So when the Lord went out of Adam, the life went out, and the light went out.

How does this apply to us? Every person born since that time has inherited Adam's nature. We are born minus God in the spirit—dead, depraved, and darkened like our father Adam.

Thus, when we say that man was made in the image of God, we need to remember it is Adam to whom we are referring. But that image was marred and defaced by sin. The Bible says concerning Adam's children, "Adam lived an hundred and thirty years, and begat a son in his own likeness, after his image; and called his name Seth" (Genesis 5:3).

We are born, therefore, in the image of Adam rather than in the image of God. Incidentally, that's a comforting thought to me. I would hate to look around at humanity as it is and think we are all in the image of God. Surely God is in better shape than that!

This deadness to spiritual things that we inherited from Adam does not mean that every person is outwardly vile or inwardly cruel. One person's lifestyle may not be as corrupt as that of someone who seems more wicked. But both are just as dead.

When a body is dead, there may be degrees of corruption and decay, but there are not degrees of deadness. Dead is dead! All people in Adam are from the same mold, though I will agree that some may be moldier than others.

The natural man is blind to the spiritual world. Because of this deadness and blindness, the natural man has no appreciation of spiritual things. Look again at Paul's words: "But the natural man receiveth not the things of the Spirit of God: for they are foolishness unto him" (2:14). The word "receiveth" here means to welcome as one would welcome a house guest. The natural man, therefore, has no welcome for Christ or for the things of God.

We need to be clear in our understanding here. This does not necessarily mean that the natural man may not enjoy coming to a religious service. He may thrill at the great music. His aesthetic nature can appreciate sunlight streaming through a stained-glass window. He can be stirred by the oratory of a gifted pastor. He may receive great comfort from the warm handshake of friendly people who congregate together.

Yet he does not truly welcome the message of God in his spirit. He does not surrender to Christ. Satan knows this and therefore is not against religion as such. He would just as soon send a man to hell from the pew as from the gutter.

Paul amplified the natural man's lack of appreciation for spiritual things when he wrote, "For the preaching of the cross is to them that perish foolishness; but unto us which are saved it is the power of God" (1 Corinthians 1:18). The natural man does not know the real meaning of the cross, which is at the heart of our faith.

Even if he could get there in his natural state, heaven would be a form of hell for the natural man. Some people who think they want to live forever don't even know what to do on a rainy afternoon! What would a person with no appreciation for the things of God do in heaven for all eternity?

Not only does the natural man have no appreciation for spiritual things, he has no comprehension of them: "Neither can he know them, because they are spiritually discerned" (2:14).

What good is a television set if the tuner is broken? No program can be received. The natural man has no spiritual apparatus, as it were, to receive divine impulses. He may hear the words, but he never really gets the message.

Nicodemus was an educated man, a ruler in Israel. But Jesus told him one night that he had to be born again before he could see or perceive the kingdom of heaven (John 3:3).

When I talk with a natural man about Jesus Christ and he says, "I just don't see it that way," I do not argue with him. Why scold a blind man for not seeing? Our job is to bear witness to Christ, then pray that God in His mercy will turn the light of His revelation onto the darkened spirit of the person involved.

A person in this condition is bound to this material world, which compounds the tragedy of life without God. Because the natural man has no appreciation for the spiritual world, he lives basically for the same things that an animal lives for—a self-gratifying, materialistic level of living without the miracle of a birth from above.

Whenever I meet a natural man, my heart yearns to say, "There is more—so much more!"

Doing What Comes Supernaturally

The second category of humanity that Paul described is the spiritual man. What are the marks of the spiritual man, the person who is living a supernatural life?

First, as the name implies, *the spiritual man lives by the Spirit.* "We have received, not the spirit of the world, but the spirit which is of God; that we might know the things that are freely given to us of God" (2:12).

He that is spiritual is simply the one who has received the Spirit of God. Because of this, he has received life. He has been

69

born from above. He is not merely a natural man who has been improved. Rather than a tadpole who has finally turned into a frog, he is more like a frog who has been transformed into a prince by the kiss of God's grace. Christians are not merely nice characters. They are *new* creatures.

We must remember, too, that salvation is a matter of receiving Christ through His Spirit into our hearts. It is not merely getting our sins forgiven. Forgiveness is necessary, but it just sets the stage for salvation—the entrance of Christ into our lives. Nor does salvation merely mean going to heaven when we die. That is wonderful, but heaven is the by-product of salvation. Salvation begins with getting the Lord, the life, and the light back into our deadened spirits.

Second, *the spiritual man learns from the Spirit.* He is given supernatural insight into the things we have been freely given by God. Paul continued, "Which things also we speak, not in the words which man's wisdom teacheth, but which the Holy Ghost teacheth; comparing spiritual things with spiritual" (2:13).

"We have received . . . the Spirit . . . that we might know," Paul said. There are some things that can only be known through the illumination of the Holy Spirit. The human spirit becomes the organ of spiritual knowledge. The Lord reveals spiritual truth to the human spirit. Of course, the mind and the emotions come into play, but they depend on the revelation that the human spirit has received from the Lord.

The One Who reveals God's truth to the human spirit is the Holy Spirit. I must always keep this in my mind and heart when I preach. How important it is that I depend upon Him. For while I can *preach* truth, only the Holy Spirit can *impart* truth. An intellectual pursuit of the Bible is important. But remember, the mind can only help us understand what God has revealed to us by His Spirit.

When God wants to illumine man, the lamp He uses is the human spirit. But the oil that feeds that lamp is the Holy Spirit. How wise we would be if we would learn to burn the oil of divine illumination rather than the wick of human intuition, which quickly burns out and leaves only so much smoke.

Third, *the spiritual man is liberated through the Spirit.* "But he that is spiritual judgeth all things, yet he himself is judged of no man. For who hath known the mind of the Lord, that he may instruct him? But we have the mind of Christ" (2:15–16).

How is the spiritual man liberated? He is no longer chained in the prison of this world's system. He sees right through it. He judges, or discerns, all things. The word "judgeth" is a legal word that implies an examination made upon the basis of illuminated insight and knowledge.

Because of the Holy Spirit, the value system of the spiritual man is operating aright. He is set free from the bondage that enslaves the thinking of the natural man. This truth sets the spiritual man free.

The last half of verse 15 makes it clear that the spiritual man will forever be a puzzle to the world. The things that motivate the natural man do not motivate the spiritual man. He marches to the beat of a different drummer. "Wherein they think it strange that ye run not with them to the same excess of riot, speaking evil of you" (1 Peter 4:4).

Don't feel, however, that the spiritual man is an oddity. He is not odd, just different. Whatever is odd about a Christian was probably odd about him before he got converted. Yet there will be an exciting distinctiveness that marks the liberated saint. The world will be puzzled at the victory that is ours.

Doing What Comes *Un*naturally

There is yet a third kind of person that Paul mentioned. This person was once spiritual but is now known as carnal or fleshly. I call him unnatural. Why? Because he is a strange mixture. He is neither fish nor fowl. He has truly been saved, for Paul called the carnal believers at Corinth his brethren. But this strange creature looks and acts much like an unsaved person. What are the marks of a carnal Christian?

The carnal Christian is deformed. "And I, brethren, could not speak unto you as unto spiritual, but as unto carnal, even as unto babes in Christ" (3:1).

Paul said the carnal Christian is like a baby who has never grown up. There is a legitimate babyhood—who doesn't love a baby? What a delight came into our home when God sent each of our children. It was a thrill when they first said, "Dada." But if my grown son were to speak that way to me today, I would not be amused at all.

In the physical realm, when a child fails to develop, the parents do not judge or condemn that child if there are physical reasons. They only pour more love and care into that precious life.

But it is quite another matter when for no reason at all we do not develop and grow spiritually. How sad it is when we have all that we need to grow and yet, because of stubbornness, ignorance, laziness, or sin, we are the spiritual counterpart of a gray-headed baby. We are spiritually deformed. It is one thing to be childlike; it is quite another thing to be childish.

The carnal Christian is not only deformed but dependent. "I have fed you with milk, and not with meat: for hitherto ye were not able to bear it, neither yet now are ye able" (3:2).

72

Paul said that, like a little baby, the carnal Christian must be fed a milk diet. There is nothing wrong with milk for the newborn, but there are so many more good things to taste and enjoy for the adult!

Technically, milk is predigested food. Carnal Christians expect a pastor to bottle-feed them on Sundays and then burp them on their way out of the sanctuary.

Because of his weak digestion and his spiritual dependency, the carnal Christian never grows in his theology much beyond "Hell is hot, heaven is sweet, and Jesus saves." Thank God that these things are true, but there is so much more to know and enjoy about the Lord Jesus Christ. While the spiritual man is sitting down to a juicy, spiritual steak with all the trimmings, the carnal Christian never gets beyond his milk, pabulum, and strained beets. And he even needs someone to feed him those.

The carnal Christian is also divisive. "For ye are yet carnal: for whereas there is among you envying, and strife, and divisions, are ye not carnal, and walk as men?" (3:3).

Like a spoiled brat, the carnal Christian is often the center of division and controversy in the church. I have noticed that little children are hardly ever concerned about the great issues of life. They are more apt to pout if the toast is cut straight across rather than diagonally (they want it to look like a little sailboat). In the church, there are big babies who are not really concerned about the greater matters of our faith but who can become absolutely unbending over where the organ should be placed.

The Corinthian church had gotten into petty squabbles over personalities. They had the "favorite preacher" syndrome. Some were in the Paul camp. "He is such a great theologian." Some were in the Peter camp. "He tells it like it is." Others were followers of Apollos. "Did you ever hear such oratory?"

Here are Paul's words to these big babies: "Therefore let no man glory in men. For all things are yours; Whether Paul, or Apollos, or Cephas, or the world, or life, or death, or things present, or things to come; all are yours; and ye are Christ's; and Christ is God's" (3:21–23).

Thus, we have God's three classifications of people, three kinds of human houses. These truths are not meant to put us down but to urge us on. When we know where we are, by God's grace we can begin to move to where we ought to be.

May the natural man repent of his sins and trust Christ. May the carnal man repent of his sins and enthrone Christ. May the spiritual man keep on repenting when he sins and so grow into greater maturity and an increasing enjoyment of Christ.

CHAPTER SIX

Inhabited or Inhibited?

May I ask you a few questions about yourself? Are you a Phi Beta Kappa, an All-American, Miss America, listed in *Who's Who*, voted "Most Likely to Succeed," or in the bluebook of society? If you answered yes to any or all of these questions, I have good news for you. God can still use you, though He is going to have a little more difficulty doing it.

But if, on the other hand, you have done or achieved none of the things the world prizes so highly, God delights to use you. If you have never won anything but the booby prize, God desires to get glory through you. As a matter of fact, He prefers to use ordinary people.

You'll understand why I say all of this when you read the following verses, which are crucial to our study of what it means to be a temple of the living God:

> For ye see your calling, brethren, how that not many wise men after the flesh, not many mighty, not many noble, are called: but God hath chosen the foolish things of the world to confound the wise; and God hath chosen the weak things of the world to confound the

things which are mighty; and base things of the world, and things which are despised, hath God chosen, yea, and things which are not, to bring to nought things that are (1 Corinthians 1:26–28).

Before we look at why God has chosen to do things this way, we need to deal with a practical matter. Is it humility to say you are not capable of being used of God? No; that is an insult to the mighty God who inhabits your heart! Believers sometimes stand with drooping shoulders and with apologetic voices declaring, "I just serve God in my poor, little, weak way."

Whenever I hear that I want to say, "Well, quit it! God does not want you to serve Him that way. He wants you to serve Him in His mighty, dynamic way. You are a temple of God. He lives within you. He wants to display His glory in you!" What some people call humility, I call poor posture. My question to people like this is, why should we be so inhibited when we are so inhabited?

You see, God has a wonderful plan. He is in the business of getting glory to Himself, and here is how He does it: He uses what the world calls a foolish message. "For the preaching of the cross is to them that perish foolishness; but unto us which are saved it is the power of God" (1:18).

He then chooses what the world considers to be a weak and unworthy messenger and compounds the two in the crucible of His mighty power and wisdom. He does this so that "no flesh should glory in his presence" (1:29). This way, the God who lives in the house gets all the glory, not the house!

Embarrassing Qualifications

To serve God in this mighty army of the ordinary, there are some downright embarrassing qualifications. Let's see how close we come to being admissible.

First are *the "foolish" ones*. The word *foolish* that Paul used comes from the Greek word *moros*. It is the word from which our word *moron* comes. It denotes someone who is dull, sluggish, or perhaps even somewhat silly.

So you were not at the top of your class? You hold no PhD degree? Does this mean you cannot be used? To the contrary, God is looking for someone just like you. Relationship is more important than scholarship.

Next are *the "weak" ones*. This word means physical weakness, even infirmity. Are you feeling weak and sickly? Congratulations! God is willing to do mighty things with and through your frail body. His strength will be made perfect in your weakness.

Then come *the "base" ones*. This word means of lowly birth, ignoble, without pedigree. Perhaps you are not from the aristocracy. You were not born with a silver spoon in your mouth. You may be like a seminary classmate of mine who said, "I wasn't born in a log cabin like some of the great men of our country, but I want you to know that just as soon as our family could afford one, we bought it and moved in!"

Praise God, He delights to use those who were born on the wrong side of the tracks. Don't let what the world may consider your social inferiority keep you from serving Him.

God also delights to use *the "despised" ones*. This word means those whom the world writes off as of no account. It means those who are treated with contempt and scorn. Do others look down on you and say you will never amount to anything? That is terrific! That means that when God does use you, it will be obvious to all around that He is the One Who is doing it and He, therefore, will get the glory.

Last of all, there are *the ones who "are not."* This refers to people who are completely overlooked. They do not even get to be despised. They are not considered good enough to be despised. They are not listed in *Who's Who.* They're not even listed in *Who's Not!*

Am I by any chance talking about you? Your name is never listed in the church bulletin. When people talk, your name is not discussed, either for good or evil. Do you consider yourself a nobody? Well, with God everybody is a somebody. He is looking for someone like you. Your name may not be mentioned much down here, but God wants you to make headlines in heaven.

These are the kinds of ordinary people God delights to use. Now let me make three things clear concerning God's plan to use His people.

God's Mighty Plan

First, God does not say that no one who is mighty or noble is called. He just says that not many of the world's elite will submit themselves to Him. I thank God for those wealthy, those gifted, those intellectuals who know and serve the Lord Jesus Christ.

Paul himself was one of these, in fact. This gifted, religious aristocrat had one of the most scintillating minds of all time. He was sought after, flattered, and praised by his peers. He had achieved the highest positions in the religious world and had an impeccable academic pedigree. Yet, Paul said concerning these achievements, "[I] do count them but dung, that I may win Christ" (Philippians 3:8).

A British noblewoman once told the great preacher John Wesley that she was saved by an *m*. Wesley was puzzled and asked what she meant. "God said not many noble were called. He didn't say not any," she explained.

The second thing I want to emphasize about spiritual qualifications is this: Paul is not encouraging half-heartedness, laziness, or mediocrity.

If you are a preacher or teacher with only an average IQ, you must study all the more. A preacher in Pennsylvania was noted as an expert fox hunter. An old Quaker said to him one day, "If I were a fox, I would hide me where thee could not find me."

"And where is that?" inquired the preacher.

"In thy study!" the Quaker replied.

You may be a singer with less than a great voice, but still it ought to be your ambition to make that voice sing the sweetest note it can sing for the glory of the Lord Jesus Christ.

You may not have great strength, but the important thing is that every nerve, fiber, bone, and sinew in your body be given over completely to the Lord Jesus. Let Him have every ounce and every inch. It has well been said, "It doesn't take much of a man to be a Christian—just all there is of him."

Third, remember that Paul is not talking about relying upon our own strength anyway. The secret of the whole matter is that God gives to ordinary people extraordinary power. He gave Himself *for* us in order that He might give Himself *to* us and therefore live His life *through* us. The issue is not so much our responsibility as it is our response to His ability.

God's Mighty Weak Ones

When I think of God using "foolish" things, I think of Billy Sunday. He was the best-known evangelist of his day, in many ways his era's counterpart to Billy Graham.

Sunday certainly could not be classed as an intellectual. He was a former baseball player who had only a high-school education. He used slang and had some laughable ideas. His antics on the platform scandalized some of the more refined church members of that era. One biographer called him "God's laugh at the preachers." Sunday used to say that he didn't know any more about theology than a jackrabbit knows about Ping-Pong.

One of my older seminary professors told me of going to hear Billy Sunday preach when the evangelist was in his heyday. He said that Billy carried on and performed in his usual way, but then God moved on him and he struck fire. He began to preach "hell hot, heaven sweet, judgment sure, and Jesus saves!" He then gave the invitation to "hit the sawdust trail," and multitudes came to trust Christ.

My professor said that among those who came forward was an old man with a long, white beard. For some reason, Billy Sunday became fascinated with that man's beard. He couldn't take his eyes from it. Finally, temptation overcame him, and the unpredictable evangelist went to the edge of the platform, bent over, grasped the man's beard, and pulled it several times saying, "Honk, honk!" Can you imagine that?

You and I might raise our eyebrows and say God couldn't use a man like that. But He did. Now, God did not use Billy Sunday because of these foolish things. And I do not suggest that any would-be preacher go and do likewise.

But here is the point: many a well-trained minister with all of the ecclesiastical accouterments (Dr. Sounding Brass or Dr. Tinkling Cymbal, for example) who trusts in his worldly knowledge and ability has been passed by. God in His wisdom chooses instead to use a Billy Sunday to bring glory to Himself. And how God used Billy Sunday! Literally hundreds of thousands came to Christ through his ministry.

When I consider God using the "weak" things, I remember an episode that took place in a church I once pastored. We were having what we called a "Week of Champions" to reach the young people in that area for Christ. We invited many great professional and amateur athletes to come and share their testimonies for Christ. The affair took place at the high-school gymnasium. Among those who came was the late Paul Anderson, who at that time was reputed to be the strongest man in the world. What a specimen he was. He had biceps like coconuts.

He was asked, "Were you ever a ninety-seven-pound weakling?"

He said, "Yes, when I was four years old!"

Anderson's testimony was clear and strong. He said, in effect, "If the strongest man in the world needs Jesus, so do you."

The next Sunday a young man came forward in our church service to confess Christ publicly as Lord and Savior. After visiting with him, I found that he was converted the night Paul Anderson was present.

"What was it Mr. Anderson said that touched your heart?" I asked.

"Oh, it wasn't what Paul Anderson said. It was what George Wilson said that reached me."

George Wilson? I couldn't remember which athlete he was. Then I recalled that George was a paraplegic in a wheelchair who gave his testimony during a time of open sharing afterward. He was not even a part of the official program. But he spoke of the joy of the Lord with a face shining like the noonday sun. That student said to me, "When I saw the happy expression on the face of George Wilson, I thought that if God could do that for a man in a wheelchair, perhaps He could do something for me."

I have never forgotten that episode. On a night when the strongest man in the world was present, God used a man in a wheelchair to bring a college student to Christ.

God's Noble Base Ones

And what about the "base" things? Do you remember the story of Gideon? He was about as ignoble and base as a man could be. He lived in a time of great trouble in Israel. The Midianites had overrun the land with their fierce warriors.

Gideon was threshing wheat one day when the angel of the Lord appeared and said to him, "The LORD is with thee, thou mighty man of valour . . . thou shalt save Israel from the hand of the Midianites" (Judges 6:12, 14).

Gideon must have looked over his shoulder to see whom the angel was talking to. When it dawned on Gideon that he was being called a "mighty man of valour," he quickly protested, "Oh my Lord, wherewith shall I save Israel? behold, my family is poor in Manasseh, and I am the least in my father's house" (v. 15).

What Gideon was saying was something like this: "Of all the tribes in Israel, Manasseh is the worst; of all the families in

Manasseh, my family is the poorest; and of all the kids in my family, I am the runt of the litter."

But this is just what God wanted—a man base enough that God could display His glory through him. And if you remember the story, you know that God made Gideon reduce the size of his army to only three hundred soldiers. It was then that God took a nobody general and a nothing army, defeated the Midianites, and got the glory. God has again and again chosen the base things of this world for His use.

Here is one more illustration of this exciting principle: when I think of despised things that God has chosen, I think of young David who later became the king over all Israel. The episode I have in mind is David's historic battle with Goliath of Gath.

The valley of Leah, about fifteen miles due west of Bethlehem, was the scene of the confrontation. The armies of Israel and the forces of the Philistines had been joined in battle for almost six weeks. Goliath, a monstrous giant almost ten feet tall and covered with brass armor, stepped forward and delivered his challenge to fight single-handedly with a Hebrew. He would raise his ham-like fists to heaven, blaspheme the God of Israel, and ridicule and taunt God's children. Who would want to take that challenge? Even mighty Saul was quaking in his boots.

David was there that day. He was just a lad, a teenage boy with fuzz on his chin. But there was something in David that was stirred to white-hot indignation when he heard the name of his thrice-holy God being mocked.

In the face of derision and certain scorn, David went forth to meet Goliath. He was armed with but a sling and five smooth stones.

There was a fundamental difference between David and everyone else that day. All the others were mumbling, "Look how much bigger Goliath is than we are." But David was thinking, *Look how much smaller than God Goliath is.* The others were saying, "He's too big to hit." David was thinking, *He's too big to miss!*

At this point, let's consider the scriptural account. It thrills me every time I read it:

> And the Philistine came on and drew near unto David; and the man that bare the shield went before him. And when the Philistine looked about, and saw David, he disdained him: for he was but a youth, and ruddy, and of a fair countenance. And the Philistine said unto David, Am I a dog, that thou comest to me with staves? And the Philistine cursed David by his gods. And the Philistine said to David, Come to me, and I will give thy flesh unto the fowls of the air, and to the beasts of the field. Then said David to the Philistine, Thou comest to me with a sword, and with a spear, and with a shield: but I come to thee in the name of the LORD of hosts, the God of the armies of Israel, whom thou hast defied. This day will the LORD deliver thee into mine hand; and I will smite thee, and take thine head from thee; and I will give the carcasses of the host of the Philistines this day unto the fowls of the air, and to the wild beasts of the earth; that all the earth may know that there is a God in Israel (1 Samuel 17:41–46).

Clearly, David was not intimidated by Goliath's threats. He knew that the battle was the Lord's.

The key to me is the last part of verse 46, where David declared that victory would be his and then gave us the reason: so God's glory would be made known in all the earth. Don't miss that point.

What would it have meant for God's glory that day if both the Philistines and Israel had put forth a giant, and the Israeli giant had defeated the Philistine giant? Not a thing in the world! It would have been just a good fight, that's all.

But when a despised, unheralded teenage boy with faith in God wins such a victory, everyone is forced to confess that there is a God in Israel. Do you see why God enjoys using despised things so that He will get the glory?

Because He Lives in Me

In the light of all this, let us as temples of the living God make a threefold application to our lives:

First of all, *there is a rebuke to our pride*—"that no flesh should glory in his presence" (1 Corinthians 1:29). God will not share His glory with another. How God hates the sin of spiritual pride! I have observed that God will keep using a person as long as that person keeps giving Him the glory.

Don't ever be like the woodpecker who while pecking away on a pine tree was stunned by a bolt of lightning that struck the tree and split it from top to bottom. Hardly able to believe his eyes, the woodpecker backed off and looked at the damage for a few moments. Then he flew away and came back leading nine other woodpeckers. With a great deal of swagger he said, "There it is, gentlemen, right over there!"

When we start to take the credit for what God does, He stops doing it!

Second, *there is a reckoning of our power.* "But of him are ye in Christ Jesus, who of God is made unto us wisdom, and righteousness, and sanctification, and redemption" (v. 30).

Don't ever insult God by saying He cannot use you. That is not humility—it is blasphemy! Christ is alive and well and lives in you if you have been saved. You are His temple. Therefore, do not say, "Lord, help me to use my love, my strength, my wisdom." Instead, rely on His! Remember that God gives extraordinary power to ordinary people.

Third, *there is a response in our praise.* "That, according as it is written, He that glorieth, let him glory in the Lord" (v. 31). How we ought to praise Him! What a wonderful plan it all is. The great God, who is big enough to fill His mighty universe, is small enough to live within my heart. *I am the temple of God.* He literally dwells in me. Hallelujah!

CHAPTER SEVEN

Like a River Glorious

We have already gazed at several important applications of the truth that our bodies are temples of the Holy Spirit. One is that when God truly possesses a temple, He possesses *all* of it. He cannot be relegated to a back room in His own temple.

We also saw that the overflowing, Spirit-filled life is the normal Christian life God wills for each believer, not a deluxe edition reserved for the choice few.

We have studied these and other truths from several standpoints. Since the Bible often teaches us by way of an illustration or picture, I want to take a close look at what I believe is one of the most thrilling Old Testament pictures—that of the Christian who has a river of revival flowing out of his life.

This great picture is found in Ezekiel 47:1–12, where the prophet had a vision of a river flowing out from the temple of God that will be built during the millennium. Since we are considering temple truth, let's examine these marvelous verses to see how Ezekiel's vision of the future can help us as we serve the Lord in the present.

To say the least, the writings of Ezekiel are difficult to understand. But of this I am certain: every temple designed by God in the Old Testament is in some way a preview and an illustration of the Christian believer, whose body is a temple of the Holy Spirit. With that in mind, let's turn to this great text and mine its truths.

A Mysterious Source

Ezekiel saw a river flowing out of the "house"—that is, out of the temple of God.

> Afterward he brought me again unto the door of the house; and, behold, waters issued out from under the threshold of the house eastward: for the forefront of the house stood toward the east, and the waters came down from under from the right side of the house, at the south side of the altar (v. 1).

Right away our minds should go to a startling event that took place in the ministry of Jesus, which may explain what Ezekiel was speaking about. The Feast of Tabernacles, the zenith of Israel's holy days, was coming to a climax in Jerusalem. It was a time of joyous thanksgiving at the end of the harvest season.

During the feast there were ceremonies each day at the time of the morning sacrifice, when the priests would bring a golden flask of water from the fountain of Siloam and pour the contents into a basin near the altar. This ritual symbolized God's bountiful provision for His people.[1] Jewish tradition says, "He who has not seen the rejoicing at the place of the water drawing has never seen rejoicing in his life" (*The Talmud*, Sukkah 5:1).

Imagine yourself there on the last day of the feast at the height of the ceremony. The city is filled with rapturous shouts as the white-robed priest pours out the sparkling water. At that very moment, you hear Jesus cry out with a loud voice:

> If any man thirst, let him come unto me, and drink. He that believeth on me, as the scripture hath said, out of his belly shall flow rivers of living water. (But this spake he of the Spirit, which they that believe on him should receive: for the Holy Ghost was not yet given; because that Jesus was not yet glorified) (John 7:37–39).

What a startling moment that must have been. Jesus could no longer be silent. He saw the hilarity, the joy, the shouting. He heard the sounding trumpets. But He knew how hollow it all was. His soul was stirred because He knew it was a passing moment of religious fervor and excitement. Before long, the people would go back to their same old fears, habits, and lethargy. The excitement would soon evaporate, just as the pitiful amount of water in that golden pitcher would soon be less than a vapor.

But at that moment, Jesus Christ proclaimed Himself to be the fulfillment of the symbol, offering the water of life right in the midst of the ceremony. But the people did not recognize Him—even though it was not ceremony but Christ, not ritual but reality, they thirsted for. It will be a great day in any land when people stop enduring religion and start enjoying salvation!

So Jesus, with a heart full of compassion and urgency, shouted out His great promise. John's parenthetical comment made it clear that this river of which Jesus spoke was the Holy Spirit, who would soon come to indwell God's people permanently.

Every Christian, therefore, is to have a river of refreshment and blessing flowing out of him as God's dear Holy Spirit expresses Himself through that Christian. Jesus pictured that river flowing out of a person's innermost being. Ezekiel pictured it flowing out under the threshold of the temple. The two pictures fit together beautifully. As we have seen, our innermost being is our spirit where we commune with God, just as the temple was the place of communion with God in the Old Testament.

· The ones to whom Jesus spoke—and still speaks—are the thirsty ones. Jesus prefaced His great promise with an "if." Thirst is the only prerequisite for the blessing. How thirsty are you? Those who are filled with the stagnant waters of carnality and self-love are seldom thirsty for the things of God. Even Christians who know they are empty may not be genuinely thirsty. The gasoline tank in my car has often been empty, but never once has it been thirsty.

But thank God for those who have a burning and blistering thirst and are willing to pay any price to satisfy it. We should be like the little girl who asked her mother for a drink of water three times in one night. Finally, the mother said in an exasperated tone, "If you ask for water one more time, I am going to spank you."

A while later the girl said, "Mama, when you get up to spank me, will you please bring me a drink of water?"

I believe that one reason we are unwilling to let go of the cheap toys of this world and drink of Jesus' fullness is that we have never really been that thirsty. Let a man have a burning, blistering thirst, and he will pay almost any price for water.

How wonderful that in Christ we can have an everlasting supply of deep spiritual blessing and life. Jesus told the Samaritan woman of water that would quench her thirst forever (see John 4:14). Christians are going from conferences to seminars to weekend retreats to get their cups filled. That will no longer be necessary when there is a river flowing from within us.

Ezekiel seemed to be foretelling the same thing that Jesus spoke of—a river of revival as God's flood of spiritual power flows from the cleansed temple of the believer in Christ.

Let's return to the prophet's vision in Ezekiel 47. Notice that the river Ezekiel saw had *a humble source*. It flowed from under the temple's threshold (v. 1). That is a lowly beginning. Genuine revival begins when God's people are on their faces before Him.

Next, it had *a holy source*. It flowed past the altar. Every temple had an altar, and we as God's temples are no exception. There can be no revival that does not flow past the altar. The altar speaks of sacrifice and cleansing, and we have these abundantly in Christ. When we meet God at the altar, the river begins to flow.

So often we cry out to God for revival as though we must persuade Him to send it. It is not our duty to persuade God to send revival, however. All we need to do is permit Him to send it when we come to the precious blood of Jesus for cleansing. There is no way we can bypass the altar and still receive the blessing.

This river flowing from the temple also had *a heated source*. Ezekiel noted that the river flowed from the east door of the temple. That was the door facing the sunrise. Also, it flowed from the south side of the altar. That was the sunny side. What a picture of the warmth of God's blessing. How our cold and frigid lives need to be warmed by God's love and power. Our coldness is one reason we are missing the blessings of God's revival power.

Robert Burns, the great Scottish poet, once went into a church hoping to find some spiritual warmth for the depression and chill that had settled upon him. But the church service was more like a funeral dirge held in a mausoleum. He failed to find any comfort in the congregation's coldness. So he took a hymnal and scribbled these words in it:

As cold a wind as ever blew,
As cold a church as in it but few.
As cold a minister as ever spak.
Ye'll all be hot ere I come back.[2]

A Marked Course

As Ezekiel was led into the river, this sparkling and bubbling trickle that came from under the temple threshold grew as it cascaded down the mountainside:

Then brought he me out of the way of the gate northward, and led me about the way without unto the utter gate by the way that looketh eastward; and, behold, there ran out waters on the right side. And when the man that had the line in his hand went forth eastward, he measured a thousand cubits, and he brought me through the waters; the waters were to the ankles. Again he measured a thousand, and brought me through the waters; the waters were to the knees. Again he measured a thousand, and brought me through; the waters were to the loins. Afterward he measured a thousand; and it was a river that I could not pass over: for the

waters were risen, waters to swim in, a river
that could not be passed over. (vv. 2–5).

The water was now surging in an ever-deepening and
widening course. It was a supernatural river because it grew
without any tributaries. Who can add anything to the all-
sufficiency of God's Spirit?

Note that the water was measured in thousand-cubit
increments. Ezekiel watched it go from ankle-deep to knee-
deep, from knee-deep to waist-deep, and finally from waist-
deep to a river that was over their heads—water deep enough
to swim in.

Here is a deepening work of God. The ankle-deep water
may speak of walking in the Spirit. The knee-deep water may
speak of praying in the Spirit. Water to the loins may speak
of being strong in the Spirit. The water to swim in may speak
of the mighty reviving force of the Spirit that picks us up and
sweeps us along in its fullness as it overwhelms us completely.
What a glorious thought!

Now God asked Ezekiel a question. "Son of man, hast thou
seen this? Then he brought me, and caused me to return to the
brink of the river" (v. 6). I want to see it, don't you? How I
long for an ever deeper work of the Spirit of God in my own
life. How I long for that mighty river to flow from my life into
my world.

This has been my prayer and desire for many years. As a
young would-be preacher, I knew I needed God's might and
power in my life. I also knew I was totally inadequate. I had not
heard much about the power of God available to the Christian,
but I knew I needed something.

Our home in Florida was near the field where we practiced
football. I went alone to that field one night to seek the Lord.

It was a beautiful South Florida summer night. I walked and prayed, "Lord Jesus, I want You to use me." Then I knelt down and repeated, "Lord Jesus, I want You to use me." Then, wanting to humble myself before Him, I stretched out prostrate, face down on the grass, and said, "Lord Jesus, I am Yours. Please use me."

That still did not seem low enough, so I made a hole in the dirt and placed my nose into it. "Lord Jesus, I am as low as I know how to get. Please use me." (I did not know it then, but I learned later that the English word *humble* comes from a Latin root *humus*, meaning "ground" or "earth.")

Something happened in my life that night. I didn't have ecstasies or a vision of any kind, but there was a transformation. At that time, I knew very little theology. But I would be less than honest to deny that God graciously released His power into my young heart and life. There was a great joy and a desire to share Christ with everyone.

Shortly after that, I entered college and was asked to serve as pastor of a small country church. I was nineteen years of age and utterly untrained. I am sure my preaching was greatly lacking in form and content, but God graciously and visibly worked. I was often surprised at His power. There were commitments for repentance and tears of joy from the start in that little congregation. People were brought to Christ in unusual numbers for such a small church and town. There was no mistaking the mighty hand of God.

How I thank God for answering my prayer for His fullness and power, not only back then but many times since. I am burdened, though, that so many are not seeing the deeper work of God. We are so satisfied with the status quo. The late Vance Havner said it well: "We have sacrificed depth for width. So rather than having a mighty power dam, we have a stagnant swamp."[3]

Where does this river flow? According to Ezekiel's vision, *it flows into the depressed places.* "Then said he unto me, These waters issue out toward the east country, and go down into the desert, and go into the sea: which being brought forth into the sea, the waters shall be healed" (v. 8).

The waters flowed from the temple mount downward. "These waters . . . go down." Those who have traveled in Israel know that the area where the waters were headed is 1,300 feet below sea level—the lowest spot on the face of the earth. But just as gravity causes water to seek the deep places, grace leads to the Spirit's seeking the depressed places in men's hearts.

And what depression there is in this world around us. It affects the up-and-outs as well as the down-and-outs. Many thought the collapse of communism in Eastern Europe and the former Soviet Union would rid the world of the threat of war and usher in a "new world order" of peace and prosperity. Did that happen? For most people it did not, and now even in America we are being told that the abundance we have enjoyed for generations is in dire jeopardy.

No wonder people whose hopes are pinned on this world are depressed! Some college students who entered a contest were asked to write a definition of life for the college newspaper. Here are some entries that won honorable mention: "Life is a joke that isn't even funny." "Life is a jail sentence that we get for the crime of being born." "Life is a disease for which the only cure is death."

These were not the deprived and the underprivileged. These were young people who seem to have everything—except Jesus.

A glorious river of revival needs to flow into depressed lives like these. This river needs to touch the college student without Christ, the businessman with his problems, the homemaker who is reduced to tears because of the depressing situation in which she may find herself. Oh, that this river of love and power might flow from temples like you and me into the depressed places.

It also flows into desert places. "These waters . . . go down into the desert." Ezekiel spoke of the Arabah, or the Judean Desert. Those who have seen it know how parched and barren it is. This desert speaks of dry and fruitless lives that need the bubbling waters of revival.

This barrenness is not only in the lives of the unsaved, but in the lives of some of those who name the name of Jesus. The curse of modern Christianity is the desert of dry mediocrity in which so many Christians are living. Jesus has chosen and ordained us to a life of fruitfulness and fullness. Yet the average Christian is living a life of dry devotions, fruitless faith, and barren evangelism. He needs the refreshing and reviving touch of the river of life that will cause his desert to blossom and bloom.

This river flows into the deadly places. "These waters . . . go into the sea." The sea that Ezekiel spoke of is the Dead Sea. Because the Dead Sea receives but does not give, except by evaporation, it has an extreme concentration of salt. It is 25 percent more salty than ocean water, and the magnesium bromine prevents organic life. The waters of the Dead Sea are leaden and poisonous.

Those who dwell in deadly places like this, those under the curse of death and judgment because of their sinfulness and selfishness, need the touch of the healing waters that flow from under the thresholds of God's temples—the hearts of His people.

There is indeed something deadly working in America. Americans, like the Dead Sea, have often taken in God's blessings, but we have not given. As a result, many people are asking, "Is God going to judge America?"

I am convinced that God is judging America. Look at the unthinkable natural disasters that have struck us. I was in St. Louis during the terrible days of the Great Flood of 1993 and saw the unbelievable, unstoppable power of the mighty Mississippi River at peak flood stage.

I met with a large group of believers there, and the number one question on their minds was whether the flood was a judgment from God on America. I do not know how you can draw any other conclusion, which is not to say that the people of the Midwest were being singled out.

But no nation can mock, ignore, and thumb its nose at the sovereign God of the universe and expect to escape His wrath. All God has to do to bring His judgment is to withdraw His protection and we are in trouble.

As I see runaway crime, racial hatred, economic confusion, moral compromise and perversion, and America's continuing loss of face nationally and internationally, I cannot help but feel that all of these comprise the judgment of God upon a sinful and selfish society.

America and the world need revival! Only God's mighty river can flow into the deadly places and make them live again.

A Mighty Force

What a mighty force a river is. We all saw the television images of the raging Mississippi wiping out entire towns. A river seems to be unstoppable. You can build levees against it and pile sandbags to the skies, but it keeps on flowing. You can dam it up, but it just rises higher until it overflows its banks and spreads over the land.

The only way to stop a river is to cut it off at its source. Since the river Ezekiel saw flowed from the temple of God, that is the only place where it can be stopped. It would seem that the Christian himself is the only one who can stop this mighty flow of power. God forbid that we should be guilty of restricting the waters of His love and power that should flow from us.

What a life-giving force this water is. Water is so very common but so very priceless. One writer said, "Water is used to cool engines, produce electricity, regulate temperatures. To produce one loaf of bread takes three hundred gallons. Between cattle rancher, butcher, packager, and processor, four thousand gallons of water will be used to put a pound of beef in the supermarket. The building of one automobile requires ten thousand gallons. The human body is seventy percent water. We are constantly losing this precious liquid, and if it's not replaced quickly, we will die."[4]

Notice also that where the waters flow, the trees will grow. "When I had returned, behold, at the bank of the river were very many trees on the one side and on the other," Ezekiel said (v. 7). Where these life-giving waters flow, there will be life rather than a sterile desert of death.

A healthy saint is pictured in the Bible as "a tree planted by the rivers of water" (Psalm 1:3). Therefore, a Spirit-filled believer should be like a river whose life will strengthen fellow believers. We are not to be reservoirs of truth but rivers of blessings to those around us.

And *where the waters flow, the fish will go.*

> And it shall come to pass, that every thing that liveth, which moveth, whithersoever the rivers shall come, shall live: and there shall be a very

great multitude of fish, because these waters
shall come thither: for they shall be healed;
and every thing shall live whither the river
cometh (v. 9).

Obviously, God has more in mind in this majestic passage
than mere fish. Jesus spoke of our becoming "fishers of men"
(Matthew 4:19). He was speaking, of course, of winning the
lost, but as we look at the modern church, we seem to be
catching very few fish.

One reason our nets are empty is that despite all of our
plans, propaganda, and paraphernalia we are fishing in stagnant
seas and polluted pools. What a harvest of souls there will be
when true revival comes and rivers of revival flow!

Think of the events that took place on the Day of Pentecost
in Jerusalem. Because Pentecost was such a great festival, the
city was wall to wall with people. Perhaps a million or more
Jews were present at that time. How would the early church
reach them? The believers were just 120 common people.
They had no printing presses or radio or television stations.
But they became the center of attention, and the "multitude
came together" (Acts 2:6). What an opportunity to preach the
gospel.

Why did the people come together? Because where the
river flows, the fish will go. The river of God's Holy Spirit was
flowing that day, and three thousand fish were caught in the
gospel net.

Next, *where the waters flow, the fruit will show*.

And by the river upon the bank thereof, on this
side and on that side, shall grow all trees for
meat, whose leaf shall not fade, neither shall the

fruit thereof be consumed: it shall bring forth new fruit according to his months, because their waters they issued out of the sanctuary: and the fruit thereof shall be for meat, and the leaf thereof for medicine (v. 12).

What is this succulent fruit that hangs in clusters from the bending boughs of these ever-green saints? Is it not the fruit of the Spirit?

Listen to Paul: "The fruit of the Spirit is love, joy, peace, longsuffering, gentleness, goodness, faith, meekness, temperance" (Galatians 5:22–23).

The world is hungry for fruit like this! In reality, Paul was describing the character of Jesus. Each of these characteristics is a facet of our dear Savior. We do not produce this fruit; He is "the true vine" (John 15:1). We merely bear the fruit when God's river is flowing from the temples of our bodies.

Finally, *where the waters flow, the health will glow*. Its "leaf" shall be "for medicine," the prophet recorded. Today the Body of Christ is suffering from a sickness that is a dishonor to its Head, the Lord Jesus Christ. But where the river of revival flows in full power, weak and anemic saints will vibrate with spiritual vitality and health. What a day that will be!

It is sad indeed that there should be so many spiritually sick saints when our great God has provided such miracle-producing medicine.

Dear reader, is the river of revival flowing from the temple of your body? If not, remember that Jesus said when we come to Him and drink, a river of living water will begin to flow from our innermost being. But He also said we must be thirsty in order to come. Ask Him to increase your thirst for the things of God.

Like a river glorious,
Is God's perfect peace,
Over all victorious,
In its bright increase;
Perfect, yet it floweth,
Fuller every day;
Perfect, yet it groweth,
Deeper all the way.[5]

—FRANCES R. HAVERGAL

CHAPTER EIGHT

Keeping Your House Clean

Remember those college boys I told you about back in chapter 3, the ones who wanted to smuggle a goat into their foul-smelling dormitory room? I said then that college boys may be content to live in a dirty place, but a holy God will not.

If you want the Holy Spirit of God to be at home in the temple of your body, it must be clean. Keeping your spiritual house clean is one of the most important responsibilities you have as a Christian.

One of the marks of a true Christian is that he feels dirty when he has sinned. David was a man after God's own heart, and yet he sinned grievously with Bathsheba and against her husband, Uriah. In his prayer of repentance, David cried out, "Wash me throughly from mine iniquity, and cleanse me from my sin" (Psalm 51:2).

Here was a king who lived a life of royalty, bathed in a marble tub, slept on silk sheets, and wore regal robes, and yet he felt dirty when he sinned. "Wash me . . . cleanse me," David prayed. He needed a spiritual housecleaning because of his sin.

The person who does not know the Lord will not be deeply affected by the grime of guilt. Sin may be so much a part of his nature that he's not even aware of its presence. A sow, for example, never feels dirty. To wallow is her way, even after she's been washed (2 Peter 2:22).

The difference between the saint and the sinner is not so much in whether they can sin. Any human being is capable of sinning. It is the basic attitude toward sin that makes the difference. The saint lapses into sin and loathes it. The sinner leaps into sin and loves it.

I know that in my life I have been made to feel dirty because of sin. But I came to Jesus, and just as He cleansed the temple in His days on earth, He cleansed and forgave me. He made the temple of my body and my life sparkling clean and fresh. And the ongoing efficacy of His shed and sprinkled blood is there to keep me clean.

In the first chapter of his first epistle, the apostle John gave us a marvelous lesson on spiritual housekeeping. It has been a personal guide to me, and I want to share it with you.

The Consequences of a Christian's Sin

That which we have seen and heard declare we unto you, that ye also may have fellowship with us: and truly our fellowship is with the Father, and with his Son Jesus Christ. And these things write we unto you, that your joy may be full (1 John 1:3–4).

These verses speak of the joy of fellowship with the Father and with the Lord Jesus Christ. This fellowship brings a joy that is full and complete. The great and costly consequence of sin in the life of a saint is the loss of this joy. The lights start to go out in his house, and the warmth starts to go too.

We do not lose our salvation when we sin (an important truth we will study in chapter 13). But if we persist in sin, we most certainly will lose the joy of our salvation. Hear the prayer of the repentant David: "Restore unto me the *joy* of thy salvation" (Psalm 51:12, italics added).

If you want to know whether you are backslidden and away from God, take the joy test. It's very simple. Is there in your heart this very moment "joy unspeakable and full of glory" (1 Peter 1:8)? If not, you are not in fellowship with the Father.

"Wait a minute!" you say. "No one can be happy all the time." I agree. But I did not speak of happiness. I spoke of joy. The two are not the same. Happiness depends on what happens. That's why we call it happiness. If your happenstances are good, then you are happy. If they are bad, you are unhappy.

But joy does not depend upon happenstance or circumstance. It comes from Jesus, and He does not change. "These things have I spoken unto you, that my joy might *remain* in you, and that your joy might be full" (John 15:11, italics added). Therefore, a promise of constant joy awaits us.

Happiness is like a thermometer; it registers conditions. Joy is like a thermostat; it regulates conditions. Paul said, "Great is my boldness of speech toward you, great is my glorying of you: I am filled with comfort, I am exceeding joyful in all our tribulation" (2 Corinthians 7:4). Jesus also spoke of His joy even when He was facing the cross.

There is only one thing that can steal your joy—sin! And only one kind of sin can do that—yours! It is not what others do to you that takes away your joy. It is your reaction to what they do that takes away the joy. Neither your wife, your children, nor your boss can diminish your joy. They may grieve you or cause you sorrow, but they cannot lay hands upon your joy. Only your reaction to what they do can take away your joy.

By the way, it is our reactions, not our actions, that show what we really are. I can more or less plan and control my life. But if you really want to know what I am like, watch me when someone insults me or steals my parking place. If you want to know what is inside a man, wait until someone jostles him, then see what spills out.

The loss of joy in a saint is a terrible loss. The most miserable person on earth is not an unsaved person, but rather a saved person who is out of fellowship with the Lord. When He saves us, God does not fix us so we cannot sin anymore. If He did, we would be robots. But He does fix us so that we cannot sin and enjoy it.

If you know pain (the great saints often have), there is all the more reason to know joy. It helps you to bear it.

The Concealing of a Christian's Sin

To err is human—and to try to conceal it is too! Notice how often in 1 John 1:6–10 the apostle repeated the phrase, "If we say . . ." We are going to look at these verses below. But first I want you to realize how this points out the deceitfulness of sin. There is within the human heart an inborn desire to conceal rather than confess sin.

One act of deceitfulness builds upon another. The longer sin goes without confession, the worse it gets in its concealment and deception. We get to the point that we will lie to others, to ourselves, and even to God.

Lying to others. "If we say that we have fellowship with him, and walk in darkness, we lie, and do not the truth" (v. 6). The Christian who is beginning to grow cold is tempted to put up a front. He pretends he is in fellowship with God. He wants others to think he is as spiritual as he has always been.

Moses had an encounter with God on the mountaintop. As a result, his face shone so brightly he wore a veil to hide the glory of God reflecting from his countenance.

Later, however, when the glory had faded, Moses still wore the veil. Only now he wore it not to hide the glory, but to hide the fact that the glory was no longer there. Many Christians in our churches are wearing a veil because the glory they once had from God has faded.

Lying to self. "If we say that we have no sin, we deceive ourselves, and the truth is not in us" (v. 8). Sin that is not quickly confessed is easily rationalized. "Maybe it is not sin after all." We might call it by other names—a mistake, an error in judgment, a glandular malfunction, or an environmental reaction.

The sad thing is that when we believe our own lies about our sin, we are doubly deceived. "If therefore the light that is in thee be darkness, how great is that darkness" (Matthew 6:23).

Lying to God. "If we say that we have not sinned, we make him a liar, and his word is not in us" (v. 10). If the Spirit of God says we have sinned, and we deny it, we are then lying to Him. And our lies to Him are a way of calling *Him* a liar. But for the grace of God, there would be no hope for a person who has gone this far in concealing his sin.

We need to learn to confess sin early. There is a deadly deception and an inevitable spread of sin when it is not confessed.

The Conviction of a Christian's Sin

"This then is the message which we have heard of him, and declare unto you, that God is light, and in him is no darkness at all" (v. 5). Thank God that He is light. Because of this, He turns the searchlight of His unspotted holiness onto every area of our lives. It is His light that reveals the dirt in His temple.

The wise Christian will open the doors and windows of his temple and let the Father flood him with light. Never be afraid of the light. More foolish than a child afraid of the darkness is a Christian afraid of the light. It is time for all of God's children to come out of the twilight zone and into the Sonlight.

But understand this: there is a vast difference between the Holy Spirit's conviction and satanic accusation. The nature of Satan is to accuse. The Holy Spirit does not accuse the saints; He convicts them. Many Christians are living lives of subsurface misery because they do not know the difference between the two. Just how does the Holy Spirit convict the child of God of his sin?

Legitimately. The Spirit will only convict you of un-confessed and uncleansed sin. Those sins that have been placed under the blood and have been forgiven have also been forgotten. God said, "I will remember their sin no more" (Jeremiah 31:34). Therefore, He never brings up our sin again.

The devil, however, loves to dredge up forgiven sin and accuse us with it over and over. He will repeat the saga of your past for you just as long as you're willing to listen to the replays.

One man was counseling with his pastor. He was being tormented by the ghost of guilt; some sin from his former days was haunting him. The pastor said, "Have you confessed it to God?"

"Oh, yes," he said, "I've confessed it a thousand times."

The wise pastor said, "That is nine hundred and ninety-nine times too many. You should have confessed it once and thanked God nine hundred and ninety-nine times for forgiving you."

Specifically. If Satan cannot accuse you of cleansed sin, he will accuse you of imagined sin. Some Christians are going around feeling bad in no particular spot but all over. They are not certain what they have done wrong, but they feel like they surely must have done something.

The Holy Spirit, however, is like a doctor making an examination. If there is a sin in our lives, He will put His finger on the sore spot and press hard. There will be no doubt as to where the problem is. He will speak to us and say something like, "You lied to your wife" or "You were harsh to your son" or "You are filled with envy."

Incidentally, while I was working on this book, one morning I spoke harshly to my wife. There was the pressure of a deadline, and I thought that my rudeness was acceptable. The Holy Spirit did not think so. "Adrian, go ask Joyce to forgive you."

"Lord, it was such a small thing."

"Ask her!"

"Yes, Lord." I did, and the joy came back.

When the Holy Spirit convicts, there will be no need for morbid introspection. We do not need to take ourselves apart a little piece at a time looking for sin. Just open your heart up to the light, and the Holy Spirit will do His work. If He does not convict you of some sin by name, then it is probably the devil who is accusing you.

Redemptively. Satan accuses you in order to condemn you. But the Holy Spirit convicts you that you might be cleansed. Accusation leads to despair. Conviction leads to confession, cleansing, and victory.

The Confession of Sin

"If we confess our sins, he is faithful and just to forgive us our sins, and to cleanse us from all unrighteousness" (1 John 1:9).

After true conviction, there must be true confession. The word *confess* literally means "to agree with" or "to say the same thing." Therefore, a genuine confession of sin is not simply an admission of that sin. Nor is confession something you do simply because you got caught. Along with admission of wrong, there must be an agreement with God concerning the seriousness of the sin and agreement that the blood of Christ cleanses you from it.

We must say about our sin what God says about it. We must take sides with Him against it. When we have done that, we have truly confessed it.

"Confess" is in the present tense, which means that it is to be the habitual practice of the saint. A Spirit-filled Christian is quick to confess sin when he becomes aware of it. It becomes a way of life. There is instantaneous and continual confession.

Not only should we confess *continually*, we should confess *completely*. Notice that verse 9 is plural: "our sins," not "our sin." Don't try to simplify your confession. Don't kneel and say, "I confess all my sins." When the Holy Spirit convicts you specifically, confess specifically.

Sometimes I would get a pen and paper and write down those areas where the Spirit of God has convicted me. I have to tell you, it *really* hurts to write those sins down and look at them. But it's been a good experience for me.

We sing the little song, "Count your many blessings / Name them one by one / And it will surprise you what the Lord hath done."[1] Perhaps we should also sing, "List your many failures / State them one by one / And it will surprise you just what *you have done*."

But I never stopped making my list. I would then confess my sins one by one. I claimed victory and absolute cleansing by the blood of Christ, and I tore up the list. I was careful to put it where no one else would ever find it. At the same time, I knew God forgave and forgot.

I am convinced that many of God's children never have the joy of full forgiveness because they sin retail and confess wholesale. Deal with sin completely.

Finally, confess *confidently*. Remember that our loving heavenly Father is "faithful and just to forgive us . . . and to cleanse us." He can do that because every sin you have ever committed was totally paid for at Calvary—even those you did willfully and that have caused permanent damage. Do you find that difficult to believe? By the grace of God, Jesus Christ paid for "the sins of the whole world" (1 John 2:2). Certainly that covers *your* sins, including the very worst of them.

Because of Calvary

If God did not forgive and cleanse *everything* we confess, He would be a liar (unfaithful) and a crook (unjust). But our God is "faithful and just." This is not a matter of our own feelings but of His faithfulness.

Pay close attention to that big little word *"all"* in verse 9. You'll also find it in verse 7: "The blood of Jesus Christ his Son cleanseth us from *all* sin" (italics added). There are no sins that God will not cleanse.

Hallelujah! Every stain, every spot, every blur, every blot, every blemish in your life can be washed whiter than snow. And what God calls clean, let no man call unclean. Even you do not have the right to hold back God's forgiveness of you!

It makes no difference how many times you have failed; He will still forgive. We may fail over and over in the same area of our lives. We become ashamed to come and ask God for forgiveness again. "Surely His patience must be worn out," we think. "He keeps forgiving me, but I keep failing."

What I am about to say is not meant to minimize sin. The fact may be, if you are continually failing in an area, perhaps you need to seek counsel from your pastor in order to become more consistent and victorious in Christ. But that is not the point here. I now want to tell you with all my soul that *if you have honestly confessed, He will forgive you, no matter how many times He has forgiven you in that same area before.*

After all, it may seem like many times to you. But from God's marvelous point of view, it is really like the first time you ever came to Him with that sin. Why? Because He forgot all the other times! The Scriptures assure us that He does not remember our iniquities and holds them against us no more.

I heard of a little girl who had been put to bed for her afternoon nap. Her mother was in the kitchen, cleaning up the lunch dishes. But noises from the bedroom indicated that the child was jumping up and down on the mattress, not sleeping.

"Settle down," the mother told her daughter as she peeked into the room through a slightly opened door. "You need your sleep. And besides, before you know it you'll break the lamp on the bedside table." It was a beautiful lamp, a prized possession in the family.

Minutes later the jumping resumed. Then came the predictable crash. "I'm really sorry," the little girl sobbed after her spanking as her mother cleaned up the broken glass.

When the mess had been taken out and dumped in the trash, the mother came back to the room, hugged her girl, and said, "I forgive you. And as far as the lamp is concerned, I'll never mention it to you again."

The very next day, as the mother was walking through the house, she inadvertently stepped on and crushed the daughter's favorite doll. The little girl ran over and picked up the broken form, held it close, and said, "Mommy, I forgive you, and I'll never mention it to you again."

Forgiveness is contagious. God not only cleanses you— He promises not to bring your sins up again . . . ever. When this assurance of sins forgiven becomes yours, you can forgive yourself, and others too, and never mention it again.

The message of God's Word is clear: "If we confess our sins, he is faithful and just to forgive us our sins, and to cleanse us from all unrighteousness" (1 John 1:9). Confess your sins. Clean up your house. Take the broken pieces of your sins out to the trash and dump them there. Forget them. God has. Then move out in the confidence that your house is clean!

CHAPTER NINE

Keeping Your Doors Locked

There's no doubt about it—God's provision for cleansing when His people sin is wonderful. But how much better it is if we can learn to nip evil thoughts and impulses in the bud before they become sin. Did you know that this is God's will for us? The same apostle who penned 1 John 1:9 also wrote, "My little children, these things write I unto you, that ye sin not" (1 John 2:1).

It is one thing to build a hospital at the bottom of a cliff in order to treat the people who plunge over the precipice. It is quite a different thing to build a guardrail up on the cliff! In this chapter, we want to build guardrails around our spiritual lives, strengthening God's temple—specifically, our minds—that we might function effectively in spiritual conflict.

Your mind is a valued trophy over which a fierce battle is constantly being waged. Paul likened the human mind to a citadel or a stronghold that is the focal point of a strategic war.

> For though we walk in the flesh, we do not war after the flesh: (For the weapons of our warfare are not carnal, but mighty through God to the pulling down of strong holds;) casting

down imaginations, and every high thing that exalteth itself against the knowledge of God, and bringing into captivity every thought to the obedience of Christ (2 Corinthians 10:3–5).

Notice the terms Paul used to speak of warfare concerning the thought life: "imaginations," "knowledge," and "thought." Without question, the human mind is a battlefield in spiritual matters. Mighty forces are assaulting your temple, striving for the citadel of your mind!

God wants your mind because He wants you. You are His temple. You have been bought with a price. It is quite obvious that if He does not control your thoughts, He will not control His temple. The command to every Christian is to "love the Lord thy God . . . with all thy mind" (Matthew 22:37).

But why is the human mind so important? Simply because we become what we think about. (I sometimes think it's a wonder I didn't turn into a girl back in high school!) "For as [a person] thinketh in his heart, so is he" (Proverbs 23:7). This verse tells us that the thought is the father of the deed. An old proverb puts it this way: "Sow a thought and you reap a deed. Sow a deed and you reap a habit. Sow a habit and you reap a character. Sow a character and you reap a destiny."

The whole process starts in the area of thought—in the mind itself.

Satan's Desire

It goes without saying that Satan wants your mind. "But I fear, lest by any means, as the serpent beguiled Eve through his subtilty, so your minds should be corrupted from the simplicity that is in Christ" (2 Corinthians 11:3). A corrupted mind—what a horrible state! And this was written to the *saints* at Corinth! Satan wants to capture, control, and corrupt the thought life of the children of God, as well as that of the unsaved.

Further, the devil knows he can disgrace the testimony of a sincere Christian and bring heartache and ruin if he can first capture his control center—the mind. If Satan can get us to *think* a wrong thing, it is likely he will be able to push us to *do* a wrong thing.

The enemy is aware that God destroyed the entire civilization of Noah's day because of evil imaginations.

> And God saw that the wickedness of man was great in the earth, and that every imagination of the thoughts of his heart was only evil continually. And it repented the LORD that he had made man on the earth, and it grieved him at his heart. And the LORD said, I will destroy man whom I have created from the face of the earth; both man, and beast, and the creeping thing, and the fowls of the air; for it repenteth me that I have made them (Genesis 6:5–7).

Indeed, Satan knows the awesome destructive power of the corrupted mind.

Satan's Devices

The devil has a well-laid plan—a strategy, if you will—to wreak havoc on our thought life. We need not guess what Satan's strategy is, for Paul has said, "We are not ignorant of his devices" (2 Corinthians 2:11). Paul had pulled the veil of darkness off of the enemy and exposed his methods. These methods can be summarized under two major headings.

First, *Satan blinds the mind of the unsaved.* As the god of this age, Satan has "blinded the minds of them which believe not, lest the light of the glorious gospel of Christ, who is the image of God, should shine unto them" (2 Corinthians 4:4).

A spiritually blinded mind is one that cannot see or perceive spiritual truth. Someone who is in this condition needs to have his eyes opened to Christ. This explains why Jesus said, "Except a man be born again, he cannot *see* the kingdom of God" (John 3:3, italics added).

A young man who was a gifted communicator wrote to a newspaper in a Florida city to tell its readers why he was an atheist. It seemed he had dipped his pen in acid. He concluded his letter to the editor by saying, "When people finally stop praying to a non-existent God to save them from a non-existent hell, then maybe one more time the world will be populated by men rather than sheep."

Sometime later, that young man was given the good news of Christ by a Spirit-filled Christian who had prayerfully asked God to open his friend's blinded eyes. God, in mercy, broke through the midnight darkness of this young atheist's mind with a shaft of gospel sunlight. He was born again and could finally see.

I spoke to him shortly after his conversion. He wanted to become a baptized member of our church. He said, "Pastor Rogers, it's so amazing what has happened to me. Before God opened my heart, I was so sure He did not even exist. But now all of that has changed, and I can hardly remember the argument I used for my atheism."

Don't scold a blind man for not seeing. Pray for him. Bind the powers of darkness and loose the powers of light by your prayers of intercession. Claim this promise: "I will give unto thee the keys of the kingdom of heaven: and whatsoever thou shalt bind on earth shall be bound in heaven: and whatsoever thou shalt loose on earth shall be loosed in heaven" (Matthew 16:19).

Second, *Satan corrupts the minds of the saved*. Don't think that salvation means automatic immunity from satanic attack on your mental fortress. We have already noted Paul's deep apprehension concerning Satan's activity among the Corinthian believers (see 2 Corinthians 11:3 above).

Because Christians can have corrupted minds, there are saints across the world filled with anxieties and fears. Chilling inner doubts have come to hide the star of hope. Impurities—unclean pictures—are hung on the walls and corridors of the mind. Cares and worries wear away the health like sand wears away or paralyzes machinery. Deceptions and false doctrines neutralize and destroy the faith and testimony of the saints. This is the tragedy of corrupted minds!

Unguarded Doors

You might ask, "How does the devil gain entrance into a Christian's thought life?" He comes in through unguarded doors. The Great Wall of China did not keep out the enemy. All that was necessary was to bribe a gatekeeper and the enemy came in. I want to mention three unguarded doors through which Satan enters the citadels and corrupts the minds of God's children.

The perverse mind. Unconfessed, harbored sin in any life is the devil's open door.

> Be renewed in the spirit of your mind; and . . .
> put on the new man, which after God is created

in righteousness and true holiness. Wherefore putting away lying, speak every man truth with his neighbour: for we are members one of another. Be ye angry, and sin not: let not the sun go down upon your wrath: neither give place to the devil (Ephesians 4:23–27).

Look at that last phrase again. Paul's thought is this: when any Christian allows the sun to set on his sin, he has given the devil a place from which to work. It's like going to bed and leaving the back door of your house wide open with the light on! The devil's place of entry is unconfessed sin, which in this case is anger. This becomes a foul nest from which Satan can hatch his hellish ideas and a stronghold from which he hurls his fiery darts of doubt. Unconfessed sin becomes Satan's legal ground from which he will not budge. By harboring unconfessed sin, the Christian can give Satan access to his house, a place to bed down.

Look at the remaining verses of Ephesians 4 and you will see that this sin may be an attitude ("anger," "bitterness," "wrath," "malice") as well as an act. Have you given the enemy easy access to your mind? Unconfessed sin is a very dangerous matter for the child of God.

The passive mind. Another door many Christians have opened to Satan is a mind that is not aggressively controlled and kept by the believer. Our minds are to be actively guarded, never wandering or passively neglected. Solomon wisely warned, "Keep thy heart with all diligence; for out of it are the issues of life" (Proverbs 4:23).

What does it mean to "keep" your mind or heart? It means to guard it, control it, and never release it to anyone or anything other than the Lord. If you become passive and fail to think for yourself, a foreign power will take up the slack. Ungodly thoughts will be planted in your heart and mind.

John made it clear that Judas was thinking Satan's thoughts when he betrayed Jesus: "And supper being ended, the devil having now put into the heart of Judas Iscariot, Simon's son, to betray him . . ." (John 13:2).

It is true that Judas, the son of perdition, was void of spiritual life. But Satan also has the power to put suggestions into the minds of God's children. I am amazed at the willingness of so many people to throw open the doors of their minds by passivity. This is the technique of the New Age movement. If you want to make contact with the spiritual forces within and around you, say the New Agers, you must surrender your mind to these forces and welcome them. Anyone who does this will make contact with spiritual forces all right, but it will be contact with the powers of darkness.

You wouldn't open all the windows and doors of your house and then go to sleep at night, just to see what might come in, would you? Who in his right mind would welcome unscrutinized guests?

Christian friend, never turn your conscious mind over to anybody or anything except the Lord. Keep it with all diligence. Spiritism, hypnotism, yoga, channeling, and other New Age forms of phony spirituality are merely unlocked doors and opened windows. Do not be foolish enough to open yourself up to them.

Even amusement can lead to passivity. It is interesting to consider what the word *amuse* really means. "Muse" means to think, but when we add the negative prefix *a* (not), it means *not* to think. When we are being amused, we are not really thinking. Our minds are in neutral and are bypassed.

121

It's amazing how careless people are when it comes to what they allow their minds to be exposed to. For example, some viewers sit in front of the television for hours, undiscerning victims of garbage programming. According to some media experts, an eighteen-year-old has watched twenty-five thousand hours of television—including literally thousands of murders.

Many of today's most popular television programs are situation comedies that make a mockery of sin. Harmless, you say? Not at all! The devil knows that once you have laughed at sin, it is difficult to think seriously about it anymore.

God has warned that His children should always have control of their minds, even when they worship Him. God does not work by putting the Christian into a blind trance or an unthinking stupor. His method is not to step outside of your mind or do an end-run around your intellect. He renews your mind and uses it.

We may meditate as Christians, but our meditation must be centered on Christ. We are to gird up the loins of our minds. "Thou wilt keep him in perfect peace, whose mind is *stayed* on thee" (Isaiah 26:3, italics added).

The polluted mind. The use of drugs and intoxicants is the third unguarded door through which Satan slips to corrupt the thought life.

The Scriptures issue clear warnings against sorcery. The word itself is a translation of the Greek word *pharmakeia*, from which we get our word *pharmacy*. It means one who enchants with drugs. Drug abuse is a form of instant insanity that opens the door to mind control by the enemy.

Here, I mean more than illegal drugs. Any beverage containing alcohol is probably the most dangerous drug in America. We are told that each year alcoholism is one of the leading causes of death in this country. According to one estimate, 18 million Americans are addicted to alcohol. A home resource on medical disorders lists twenty-four conditions that are either caused by or aggravated by the consumption of alcohol.[1]

That's bad enough, but of course this list does not include the most damaging effect of alcohol—the spiritual devastation it causes. And I am not just talking about the heavy drinker. Even the so-called social drinker can be prey to the evil effects of a drug that one former alcoholic called "dirty, vicious, and brutal." With alcohol so widely accepted, even within the church, the danger is that much greater.

One man bragged that he drank vodka so no one could smell liquor on his breath and know he was drinking. A friend said, "If I were you, I would drink something else. It would be better for them to know you are drunk than to think you are stupid."

Not only is it stupid to give our minds over to pollution, it is sad. Many Americans who claim to be Christians have opened the door to mind control by the devil through sorcery or the use of drugs. Beware of the polluted mind!

Satan's Defeat

Thank God that it is possible for His children to actively recapture the citadel of their minds. If you have misused your mind, I have good news and hope to offer. It is found in the verses I quoted at the outset of this chapter, 2 Corinthians 10:3–5.

Clearly, according to Paul, there is victory for the child of God. But please notice that "carnal" weapons are not sufficient for this spiritual battle. The battle for the mind will never be won by education, psychology, psychiatry, or positive thinking.

These all have a proper place, but one might as well throw snowballs at a Stealth Bomber as to try to dislodge Satan's thought patterns with such carnal weapons.

If "the weapons of our warfare are not carnal, but mighty through God to the pulling down of strong holds," what are those weapons? I want to mention three mighty weapons that will secure and guard the mind of the believer who has suffered invasion by the enemy.

For the perverse mind, there is repentance. Don't ever think that only the unsaved need to repent. Jesus' last word to the church was not the Great Commission. It was, "Repent." Five of the seven churches of Asia Minor that the risen Lord addressed in Revelation 2–3 were commanded to repent.

The Greek word for repentance is *metanoia*, which literally means "a change of mind." There is no way to deal with the perverse mind but to change it. The sin that has become Satan's foul nest and legal territory must be uprooted and removed. It will not do you much good to try and keep your house in order if Satan occupies the rumpus room!

Repentance always leads to confession, confession leads to cleansing, and cleansing takes away the place given to the devil (Ephesians 4:27). How wonderful when the cleansing tides of Calvary wash over the soul and the fresh breeze of the Spirit sweeps through the mind.

Why is it that we modern Christians are willing to try almost everything today but good old-fashioned repentance? Are there areas of satanic stronghold in your mind right now over which you need to exercise mind-changing repentance? Is God the Holy Spirit telling you that you need to repent?

Turn from these things *now*. If not, I don't think there is much else I can say to you in this book that will help. Come to Christ with a soft heart, and repent of your sins—that is the only answer.

For the passive mind, there is resistance. "Submit yourselves therefore to God. Resist the devil, and he will flee from you" (James 4:7). Why should you resist? Because Satan will not give up anything or anybody without a struggle.

And how can you resist? Do what you know is right. Say no to sin. Make certain that every sin is confessed. Make sure that you have, through God's power, taken back every stronghold you yielded. And then ask the Lord to rebuke Satan (see Jude 9). Remember, the devil now has no legal right. He *must* flee.

You may also need to say, "I resist the enemy in the name of Jesus. He has no right or authority in my life. My body is the temple of the Holy Spirit. I am bought with the price of the blood of Christ. The devil cannot trespass on my Father's property. Lord, rebuke him!"

For the polluted mind, there is renewal. Minds that have been damaged and distorted can be made over. New thought patterns can and must be established. Listen to these marvelous promises:

> Be renewed in the spirit of your mind (Ephesians 4:23).

> I beseech you therefore, brethren, by the mercies of God, that ye present your bodies a living sacrifice, holy, acceptable unto God, which is your reasonable service. And be not conformed to this world: but be ye transformed by the renewing of your mind, that ye may prove what is that good, and acceptable, and perfect, will of God (Romans 12:1–2).

God will renew your mind after you repent and resist. This will be done as you change the focus of your attention. Remember that we become what we think about.

Now here's the exciting part: God has so engineered your mind that you cannot think two thoughts at one time. So if you are thinking what is right, you cannot be thinking what is wrong.

Paul stated this so beautifully:

> Finally, brethren, whatsoever things are true, whatsoever things are honest, whatsoever things are just, whatsoever things are pure, whatsoever things are lovely, whatsoever things are of good report; if there be any virtue, and if there be any praise, think on these things (Philippians 4:8).

Let me give you this word of advice about the renewed mind. Do not try to avoid thinking wrong thoughts. That never works. For example, for the next thirty seconds, whatever you do, don't think about an elephant. If my guess is right, that's about all you *will* think about for the next thirty seconds. Why? Because you are trying *not* to think about an elephant. Right?

Here's the way to do it. Just get up each morning and bathe your soul in the presence of Jesus. Talk with Him, first off, in prayer.

Then saturate your mind with His Word. "Let the word of Christ dwell in you richly in all wisdom; teaching and admonishing one another in psalms and hymns and spiritual songs, singing with grace in your hearts to the Lord" (Colossians 3:16). Commit your day to Him. Before long, it will become evident that God is renewing your mind.

The doors of your temple can be shut to the enemy while its windows are open to the Lord!

CHAPTER TEN

A House of Prayer—
Not a Den of Thieves

As temples of the Holy Spirit, we should be houses of prayer.

The importance of prayer was uppermost in the Lord Jesus' mind as He cleansed the temple in Jerusalem. He then stood guard over the temple, not allowing anyone to defile it. And He had a message: "He taught, saying unto them, Is it not written, My house shall be called of all nations the house of prayer? but ye have made it a den of thieves" (Mark 11:17).

Anything that distracts us from vital prayer is a treacherous thief. It steals from us the blessings the Father longs to bestow, and it takes from the Father the glory He so richly deserves.

How foolish we are to allow ourselves to be so robbed. If we are to keep our temples clean and well-protected, we desperately need to learn the art and the discipline of prevailing prayer. Prayer is so fantastic because it links us with the Almighty God in a miraculous way. Prayer can do anything God can do, and God can do anything. That may sound astounding, but read on.

One day as I was meditating, one of the most electrifying thoughts I have ever had came into my heart. I cannot fully explain the impact that it made on me. Yet, this thought is so simple and presumably so well-known that I almost hesitate to tell you about it. But here it is: *God hears and answers prayer!*

Oh, you say, every Christian knows that. Yes, so did I—in my head. But somehow I suddenly saw the truth of that truth, if you will, and it shook me to my very foundation.

I thought, *If this is true, and it is, then the one thing above everything else I should learn to do is to pray.* There can be no greater achievement than a vital prayer life. I challenge you to stop and consider the impact of this thought with me—that we as mortals can link our nothingness with God's almightiness through prayer. I say it again: what fools we are if we do not learn to pray!

Failure to pray is a tragedy, but it is more than a tragedy. It is a sin. God's Word says in 1 Samuel 12:23, "As for me, God forbid that I should sin against the LORD in ceasing to pray for you: but I will teach you the good and the right way."

With this in mind, I want us to see what Jesus taught about prevailing prayer. Do not let your familiarity with the following passage keep you from giving it the full attention of your heart and mind. What an amazing passage it is. The more we look at it, the more we see. It is sweet to the child, perplexing to the scholar, and beneficial for every one of us.

> After this manner therefore pray ye: Our Father which art in heaven, Hallowed be thy name. Thy kingdom come. Thy will be done in earth, as it is in heaven. Give us this day our daily bread. And forgive us our debts, as we forgive our debtors. And lead us not into temptation, but deliver us from evil: For thine is the kingdom, and the power, and the glory, for ever. Amen (Matthew 6:9–13).

Before Jesus gave this lesson on prayer, He had warned against praying only to be seen by men.

I heard of a young lawyer who had just opened up a brand-new office. He was seated behind his shiny new desk, eagerly awaiting his first client. Soon he heard footsteps in the hall and then a hand on the doorknob. Wanting to look important he pretended to be busy, so he picked up the telephone and carried on a fake conversation.

"Yes, yes, I'll have my secretary tend to that. I have a very heavy schedule. Call me back in a few days." He motioned toward the door as if to say, "Come in, come in." The stranger entered the office, listening to one end of the high-level conversation.

Finally, the receiver was put back on the hook, and the lawyer turned to what he hoped was a prospective client. "Now, what may I do for you?"

The man answered calmly, "I'm from the phone company, and I came to connect your telephone."

So much of our praying is like that. We are praying to be seen by men, but no one is on the other end of the line. Wouldn't you like to quit playing games and get down to serious business in this matter of prayer? Let's allow the Lord Jesus, the Master Teacher, to show us how as we examine His wonderful model of prayer.

The Person of the Prayer

Our Father. Notice how Christ's model prayer begins. Right away we learn that vital prayer is not an empty repetition of words but is rather a child talking with his Father. Because this is so, several other truths come quickly to mind.

We must be children of God in order to pray with effectiveness. Not everyone has the right to call God "Father." Only those who have been born into His family have that right.

Someone may protest, "Wait a minute. God created everybody, so God is the Father of everybody." I beg to differ. He is not the Father of everybody. God does not become Father by creation. He created cats and dogs, flies and frogs, but He is not their Father. He is only their Creator.

God has made it clear in the Scriptures that some human beings are not His children. Jesus said of the unconverted Pharisees, "Ye are of your father the devil" (John 8:44). We become children of God and can call Him "Father" only when by faith we receive Christ as our Lord and Savior and are born into God's family. The apostle John made this clear when, concerning Jesus, he said, "He came unto his own, and his own received him not. But as many as received him, to them gave he power to become the sons of God, even to them that believe on his name" (John 1:11–12).

If God is your Father, how simple and natural it ought to be for you to pray. Some think that we have to use the language of Shakespeare in order to pray. This is not so! Nor do we need to repeat certain prayers over and over. Jesus said, "When ye pray, use not vain repetitions, as the heathen do: for they think that they shall be heard for their much speaking" (Matthew 6:7).

Suppose when my daughter was still at home she had met me when I came home one day and said, "Oh, hail thou eminent pastor of Bellevue Baptist Church. I beseech thee that thou wouldest grant to thy daughter, whom thou lovest, some financial assistance that she may sojourn to yon apothecary for some cosmetical necessities."

I think I would have said, "Huh?"

But my daughter wouldn't have done that. She would simply have said, "I love you, Daddy. I'm so glad you're home. By the way, I need five dollars to get some things at the drugstore."

Remember, God is your Father. The Holy Spirit has even taught you to pray, "Abba, Father" (Romans 8:15). *Abba* is an Aramaic word that is very close to our word *Daddy*. It is one of the first words formed upon the lips of a little baby. How thrilling to know that if you are God's dear child, you can come with such intimate confidence as to call Him "Abba, Father."

The Purpose of the Prayer

Thy will be done. This phrase tells us immediately that prayer has one major purpose: to seek and to secure the will of God. Prayer is answered only when it is offered in the will of God. "This is the confidence that we have in him, that, if we ask any thing according to his will, he heareth us" (1 John 5:14). Someone has wisely said, "Nothing lies beyond the reach of prayer except that which lies outside the will of God."

Someone may ask, "Do you mean that in my praying I am restricted to the will of God?" Yes, but do not be concerned about that! For us to worry about being restricted by the will of God is like a minnow worrying about being hemmed in by the Atlantic Ocean.

Praying in the will of God does not mean fewer blessings for us but more and greater blessings. God wants for us what we would want for ourselves if we only had enough sense to want it. We should never fear the will of God.

Remember that prayer is not some exercise whereby we try to bend God's will to fit our wills. Prayer is not talking God into doing something that He ordinarily would not want to do.

Prayer is the thrilling experience of finding God's will and then asking Him for it.

That brings into focus a very key question: how do we know God's will? Obviously, God's will is made known in a general sense as we read the Bible, but there are so many specific things that the Scriptures do not touch upon. There is no Scripture that tells us what job to take, whom to marry (incidentally, proper prayer would help avoid many divorces— and quite a few marriages), or what school to attend.

The secret of knowing God's will in prayer is not only to know the Bible and let its truth abide in us, but to be very, very sensitive to the leading of the Holy Spirit. Because you are a temple of God and a house of prayer, God's Holy Spirit abides within you and *will help you pray* (Romans 8:26–27). The Bible calls this "praying in the Spirit."

> Praying always with all prayer and supplication in the Spirit, and watching thereunto with all perseverance and supplication for all saints (Ephesians 6:18).

> But ye, beloved, building up yourselves on your most holy faith, praying in the Holy Ghost(Jude 20).

When we pray we are to pray to the Father, through the Son, in the Spirit. What a glorious partnership there is between the Holy Spirit and the human spirit. He teaches us the will of God and helps us to pray as we ought. The Holy Spirit, as our Helper, wants to think through our minds, feel through our hearts, speak through our lips, weep through our eyes, and express Himself through our spirits.

One of the greatest truths I have ever learned about prayer is this: the prayer that gets to heaven is the prayer that starts in heaven. All we do is close the circuit.

I once heard someone give this definition of prayer: "Prayer is the Holy Spirit finding a desire in the heart of the Father and then placing that desire into our hearts. The desire is then sent back to heaven in the power of the cross."

This is why we must learn to wait before the Father in meditation and openness when we pray. So often we simply rush into the presence of God and say, "Listen, Lord, your servant speaks" rather than saying, "Speak, Lord, your servant is listening."

Are you listening? Are you honestly seeking to know and do the will of God? Man's ruin began in the Garden of Eden, when the spirit of the first Adam said, "Not Thy will, but mine, be done."

Man's rescue came in another garden when the last Adam said, "Not my will, but thine, be done" (Luke 22:42).

The Spirit of the Lord Jesus is the Spirit that should characterize our praying.

The Provision of the Prayer

Give us this day our daily bread. Surely we may ask for what we need. While we are not to pray selfish prayers, we certainly may pray for personal needs. Our Father is concerned with every need we have.

Remember that this model prayer is but a guide for praying. I do not believe that Jesus meant we should ask only for bread. What He did mean was that we should bring all of our needs to the Father and ask Him specifically for what we need.

We can pray this way because the earlier petition for God's name to be "hallowed" is a guard against mere self-seeking in prayer. If you can sincerely pray, "Hallowed be thy name," which means to regard God as holy and to make His holy name known, then you are ready to pray for your needs.[1]

Paul reminded us, "My God shall supply all your need according to his riches in glory by Christ Jesus" (Philippians 4:19). I am so very glad he did not say, "out of his riches," but "according to his riches."

A millionaire may give you one dollar out of his riches, but that is not necessarily according to his riches. The gift does not reflect what he is capable of doing. Think of the vast riches of our Father, and realize that He is ready to meet our needs according to those riches.

I am also very glad Paul did not say, "all your wants." He said, "all your need." I have sometimes wanted things I did not need; and I have sometimes needed things I did not want. For example, my dad would say sometimes, "Adrian, you need a spanking." He was quite right, but of course I did not want one.

I believe many Christians have needs that are unmet simply because they do not pray. "Ye have not, because ye ask not" (James 4:2).

When I was a student pastor in Florida, I shepherded a small church in Indian River County. You may not know it, but the best citrus fruit in all of Florida grows there. One day as I was returning to college after serving my church on the weekend, a deacon gave me several bushels of delicious oranges.

I said, "Mr. Ingram, I cannot eat all of those oranges before they spoil."

He said, "Well, take them back to college, Adrian, and give them away."

So I took the oranges back with me to college, lugged them upstairs to our tiny, second-story garage apartment, and put them in a closet.

One day shortly after that, I looked out into our backyard and saw a little fellow about seven years of age sneaking around in a suspicious manner. He was looking every way but up. (Does that remind you of anyone you know?)

I realized after a while that he was going to steal an orange from the lonely orange tree in our backyard. I decided I would let him, because he did not know that this was a sour-orange tree. In Florida, these sour-orange trees are very beautiful ornamental shrubs, but the fruit is extremely bitter. As a matter of fact, it is not fit for man or beast.

I watched that little guy as he plucked his prize. Even though I was working my way through school, I believe I would have given a dollar to see him take that first bite.

Now the irony of the whole matter is this: had he only knocked on my door and asked, "Mister, may I have one of those oranges?" I would have said no. But then I would have loaded him down with more of the very best oranges than he could carry.

When we get to heaven, I wonder if the heavenly Father will not bring us to some huge cosmic closet and say, "Look in there. Do you see all of those things? They are the blessings I longed to give you, but you never asked. You were enjoying the bitter fruit of your own scheming and wisdom rather than asking Me for what is best."

Let us learn to ask the Father for the things we need. Remember, there is nothing big enough to concern us that is too small to concern Him. Ask Him for your needs.

The Pardon of the Prayer

Forgive us our debts. Powerful prayer must come from a clean heart. Jesus taught us to pray for daily forgiveness just as we pray for daily bread. Since we have already talked at length about confession and repentance, let me just highlight a few things by way of review.

The reason many of our prayers are not answered is that we are not including confession and repentance with our petitions. A prayer from a dirty heart is a prayer not answered.

We like to quote the Bible's prayer promises, don't we? Let me give you a prayer promise we are prone to forget: "If I regard iniquity in my heart, the Lord will not hear me" (Psalm 66:18).

Is there any iniquity that you have made peace with? Is there any sin, habit, or grudge that you have regard for? If so, for God to answer your prayer would merely be an encouragement for you to continue in that sin.

James warned all of us when he wrote, "Draw nigh to God, and he will draw nigh to you. Cleanse your hands, ye sinners; and purify your hearts, ye double minded" (James 4:8). We cannot pray effectively with dirty hands, defiled hearts, and double minds.

I am told that monkeys are captured in the South Sea Islands in an unusual way. The natives fasten a coconut with a hole in it to a tree. Some rice is then placed inside the coconut. A curious monkey will examine the coconut and see the rice inside.

He then puts his paw through the hole and grabs a fistful of rice. But with his hand now doubled up, it is too big to withdraw. The poor monkey will plead and scream as his captor approaches, but he will not release the rice so he can withdraw his hand.

136

One wise man prayed like this: "Oh, Lord, help me to cooperate with You so You won't have to operate on me." We should do the same. So many of us, it seems, would rather hold on to our sins than enjoy the freedom of a prayer life that knows no limits.

If there are sins that have made your temple a den of thieves rather than a house of prayer, pray, "Forgive me my debts." Then let go of your fistful of rice, so God can stop chastising you and start blessing you.

The Protection of the Prayer

Deliver us from evil. This phrase could be rendered, "Deliver us from the evil one." Satan is so very real. He has already made plans to sabotage your life and to hurt your loved ones. He has already dug a pit for your feet to fall into today.

His real war is with God, but he cannot get at God directly. He knows, as evil people have always known, that if you cannot harm someone, the next most effective thing is to harm someone whom that someone loves. God loves you, and therefore Satan has aimed all the artillery of hell at you. You need protection.

Your protection is provided through prayer. The prayer for deliverance from evil and temptation is preventive medicine, though we are prone to forget that. I feel certain that the reason we keep wearily asking for forgiveness for the same sins and making the same confessions is that we have not been claiming our protection from the enemy.

The reason we fall into this trap is that we remember to pray, "Forgive us," but we fail to pray, "Deliver us."

What happens is something like this: we wake up a little late. We hurry through our devotions—or have none at all.

But it's a new day anyway, and nothing has happened yet to upset us. Things are running smoothly. We catch a snatch of the newspaper and gulp down a little breakfast and dash off to work. (Why do they call it "rush hour" when the traffic moves so slowly?)

But we get our day started, and everything seems to be going just fine. Then at an unsuspecting moment, Satan tosses a bombshell into our laps, and spiritually we are blown to smithereens. (I've always wondered what a smithereen is.) We fail miserably!

At the end of the day, we try to clean up the mess. We bow before God and pray, "Forgive me my debts." And He does.

But this model prayer Jesus has given us is not a prayer for the end of the day. This is a morning prayer. Can you imagine someone coming to the end of the day and praying, "Lord, give me today my daily bread"? And then off to sleep he goes. That would be foolish. Just as in the morning we ask for the day's provision, we are to ask for the day's protection too.

I have a friend, a former professional football player, who likes to tell this story: "When I graduated from college, my coach said, 'Mike, would you help me do some scouting?' (For the uninitiated, that means to look for some prospective football players to be enrolled in college!)

"I said, 'Sure, Coach, what kind of player are you looking for?'

"He said, 'Well, there's the kind of guy that when you knock him down, he just stays down.'

"'We don't want him, do we, Coach?'

"'No, we don't. But there's the kind of guy that when you knock him down, he gets up; knock him down, and he gets up; knock him down, and he gets up; knock him down again, and he just keeps getting up.'

138

"'That's the guy we want, right, Coach?'

"'No, we don't want him either. What I want you to do is find the guy who's knocking all the other guys down. That's the guy I want.'"

I say Amen to that. I am glad God enables us by His grace to keep getting up every time Satan knocks us down. But I think it is time that God's people got off the defensive and went on the offensive. It's time Satan started fleeing from us. And he will flee when we begin the day by putting on the whole armor of God and bathing our souls in the presence and power of the Lord Jesus by claiming the protection of prayer.

The Praise of the Prayer

Thine is the glory. Notice that Jesus' prayer opens and closes on a note of praise. How appropriate. Prayer must be done in faith, and praise is the best expression of faith I know of. Praise is faith turned inside out.

When we ask God for things, that is petition. But petition without praise is unbelief. Praise without petition, however, is presumption. But when we link petition and praise together, that is power. When I ask God, and then praise God, I am believing God. Petition says, "Please." Praise says, "Thank You."

If your faith is strong, your prayer will be strong. Pray and believe and you will receive. Pray and doubt and you will do without.

How important it is, therefore, that we learn to praise. I cannot overestimate the power of praise. If your prayer life seems useless and powerless, learn to praise God.

The Bible says that God inhabits the praises of His people. He is so very near when we praise Him. Billy Sunday was right

139

when he said, "We need to jerk some of the groans out of our prayers and shove in a few hallelujahs."

Why shouldn't we offer praise? Our Father is a King! Just think about that. I have a Father who will hear me and a King who can answer me. I have the sympathy of a Father and the sovereignty of a King attuned to my prayer. Why shouldn't I offer God praise? You will discover victory when you make your temple a house of prayer and a house of praise!

CHAPTER ELEVEN

The Golden Key
of Faith

Paul's prayer for the Ephesians was "that Christ may dwell in your hearts by faith" (Ephesians 3:17). The door through which Jesus enters the human heart—and thereby makes you His temple—swings upon the hinges of grace, and faith is the key that unlocks that door.

In this chapter, I want to think with you about what I call the "golden key of faith," which opens the door of the heart to Jesus and also the door of heaven's riches to the believer. Faith is not only our house key but the key to God's storehouse.

All of God's blessings come to us through faith. Jesus said, "According to your faith be it unto you" (Matthew 9:29). Therefore, the benchmark of blessing is not according to our feelings, friends, fame, or fortune, but according to our faith. The measure of accomplishment in the Christian life is always faith.

Conversely, most of the problems in a Christian's life are caused by lack of faith. *Worry*, for instance, is the opposite of faith and is an insult to God. Worrying is like saying, "God, I don't think You can handle this one." *Loneliness* is the result of not believing in God's presence. Faith makes God's presence very real to us even when no one else is near. *Unbelief*, however, leaves us isolated even in a crowd.

Many other people are haunted by the ghost of *guilt* because they lack confidence in the full forgiveness of God's grace. Faith is our acceptance of God's acceptance of us. *Disobedience* results from lack of faith in what God has said.

It is human nature to touch the paint when the sign says, "Wet Paint." We are not quite sure it's wet, so we check for ourselves. If we truly believe the "wet paint" signs in God's Word, however, we will not so easily transgress.

The Description of Faith

The book of Hebrews contains a mighty message on this vital subject of faith, probably the most well-known description of faith in all of Scripture: "Faith is the substance of things hoped for, the evidence of things not seen. For by it the elders obtained a good report" (Hebrews 11:1–2).

To my knowledge, there is no precise definition of faith given in the Scriptures. But even though the verses above describe rather than define faith, they make clear what faith is in the life of the believer.

Faith is not positive thinking. It is not following a hunch. It is not a feeling of optimism. It is not hoping for the best. All of these may be well and good in their place, but they are not biblical faith. What is faith, then?

FAITH IS SUBSTANCE

"Faith is the substance of things hoped for." *Substance* means "solid ground." The English word gives the meaning of the Greek quite well. *Sub-stans* means there is something beneath us to stand upon. When we are living by faith, we are not walking on eggshells and Jell-O. We are standing upon the Solid Rock.

Sometimes the materialist will say, "Don't talk to me about faith. Talk about real things." He means, of course, the things that can be experienced with the five senses—the things we can see, smell, hear, taste, or touch.

But are these the only things that are real? Paul reminded us that "the things which are seen are temporal; but the things which are not seen are eternal" (2 Corinthians 4:18). Which is more real—that which is temporary or that which is eternal?

FAITH IS EVIDENCE

"Faith is . . . the evidence of things not seen." This means that faith is the *convincing proof* that God will keep His Word.

Evidence is the proof of unseen reality. There can be no evidence without the reality that gave rise to the evidence. It is so important that we understand this. If we do, we shall see the difference between real and synthetic faith.

There is a counterfeit faith today that is really nothing more than positive thinking couched in religious terms. The prophets of this synthetic faith explain it by saying, "God is able to do anything. Therefore, if you have enough faith, He will do anything you want. All you have to do is *name it and claim it.*"

That sounds good, but it bears little resemblance to biblical faith. We do not "name it and claim it." We cannot legitimately claim it until God has named it. Faith is actually our response to a revelation of God's will by His Word and His Spirit. "So then faith cometh by hearing, and hearing by the word of God" (Romans 10:17).

Believing does not make it so. "Just have faith" is silly advice if there's no object to the faith. Faith does not bring anything into existence. Faith is the evidence of things that are already in the heart and mind of God.

I cannot truly believe until a thing is settled. Anything else is but positive thinking or a wishful desire. Faith is the evidence in my heart that God has spoken.

The Dynamics of Faith

Faith is the most dynamic force in the world because it releases the hand of omnipotence. Hebrews 11:6 gives us insight into the mighty power of faith: "Without faith it is impossible to please him: for he that cometh to God must believe that he is, and that he is a rewarder of them that diligently seek him." There are three major thoughts in this verse we need to consider.

LACK OF FAITH DISPLEASES GOD

"Without faith it is impossible to please him." A lack of faith—that is, unbelief—greatly displeases God. Unbelief is a vile and wicked sin. Really, there is no greater sin. It is the parent sin. Unbelief is the sin out of which all other sins grow, the one sin that keeps a person out of heaven. Jesus said:

> For God sent not his Son into the world to condemn the world; but that the world through him might be saved. He that believeth on him is not condemned: but he that believeth not is condemned already, because he hath not believed in the name of the only begotten Son of God (John 3:17–18).

The sin of unbelief is so terrible because of what it says about the character of God. Suppose you are introduced to a group as a speaker. The master of ceremonies says many nice things about you but then adds, "There is one thing I must tell you about our speaker—you cannot believe what he says."

It would not matter then how many nice things he had said. When he said you could not be believed, he cut the taproot of your character.

It matters not how many nice things you may say about God if you do not believe Him. What difference does it make how we speak of the greatness of God or of His love when we refuse to believe He is worthy of our faith? "He that believeth not God hath made him a liar" (1 John 5:10). What a sobering thought.

Someone may protest that he cannot believe because he has genuine intellectual problems. "It is not my fault if I cannot believe," he says.

But it *is* his fault. Unbelief is a moral sin, not an intellectual problem. It starts in the heart, not in the head. It may show up in the head, but that is only a symptom of what is in the heart. "Take heed, brethren, lest there be in any of you an evil heart of unbelief, in departing from the living God" (Hebrews 3:12).

A man who held an important position in the space industry at Cape Canaveral once came to see me concerning his wife. She was suicidal, and he wanted me to counsel with her. I said I would if he would come with her. He agreed to come.

In my study, the wife poured out her story of a broken heart. She wept as she spoke of her husband's cruelty, infidelity, drunkenness, and gambling. I turned to him and asked, "Sir, are you a Christian?" Mind you, I was not asking for information but was turning the conversation toward Christ.

He threw back his head and laughed scornfully. "No, I am an atheist," he said.

"Well," I responded, "an atheist is one who knows there is no God. Do you know all there is to know?"

"Of course not," he shot back.

"Would it be generous to say you know half of all there is to know?"

"Yes, that would be very generous," he muttered.

"Then if you only know half of all there is to know, wouldn't you have to admit the possibility that God may exist in the body of the knowledge you do not have?" I asked.

"I never thought of that," he said. "Well, I am not an atheist then. I am an agnostic."

I said, "Now we are getting somewhere. Agnosticism means you don't know." (I didn't tell him that the Latin equivalent for agnostic is ignoramus!) "An agnostic is a doubter."

"Well, that is what I am, and a big one."

"I don't care what size as much as what kind. There are two kinds of doubters, you know—honest and dishonest. The honest doubter doesn't know, but he wants to know. The dishonest doubter doesn't know because he doesn't want to know. He can't find God for the same reason a thief can't find a policeman. Which kind of doubter are you?" I asked him.

His face softened. "I never really thought about it. I guess I never really wanted to know," he said.

"Did you know that there is a promise to the honest doubter in God's Word?" I asked. I then read to him these words of Jesus, who was speaking to the doubters of His day: "My doctrine is not mine, but his that sent me. If any man will do his will, he shall know of the doctrine, whether it be of God, or whether I speak of myself" (John 7:16–17).

146

I continued, "In plain English, this says that if a man surrenders his will completely, God will reveal Himself to that man." My friend was getting interested.

I then asked him, "Would you be willing to sign a statement like this: 'God, I don't know whether You exist or not, but I want to know. And because I want to know, I will make an honest investigation. And because it is an honest investigation, I will follow the results of that investigation wherever they lead me, regardless of the cost.'"

After a time of soul-searching, he responded, "Yes, I would be willing to sign a statement like that. I will do it. How do I go about making such an investigation?"

We shared further together, and I got him started reading the gospel of John with the commitment that he really wanted to know the truth and would follow any truth revealed to him regardless of the personal cost or consequences.

In a matter of weeks, he came back to my study, got on his knees, and gave his heart to Christ! In a letter I received from him years later, he said, "Dear friend, thank you for being willing to spend time with this general in the devil's army." He was then an active and vibrant lay leader in another state.

Where was this man's real problem? It was not in his head as he first thought but in his heart. When he surrendered his will, faith followed. Unbelief reveals a wicked heart.

BY FAITH WE GIVE GOD PLEASURE

"He that cometh to God must believe that he is." If unbelief displeases God, faith obviously pleases Him. We should have no greater aim in life than to please God. For if we please God, it really doesn't matter whom else we displease. Conversely, if we displease God, it really doesn't matter whom we please. But there is no pleasing God without believing Him.

Why is this so? Why is God so pleased with faith? Why didn't He just create us so that we would automatically believe in Him? Why doesn't He do something to prove Himself to us?

Have no doubts about it. If God wanted to prove Himself, He would have no difficulty doing so. He could roll back the heavens and make Himself known with a display of His grandeur, might, and glory. There would not be one unbeliever left upon the earth. However, such displays would render faith unnecessary.

One day God will reveal Himself in just that way. It will not be to save men, however, but to judge them. At that time, every knee will bow and every tongue will confess, but it will be a fearful and awful day.

In this day and age, God refuses to reveal Himself in that manner because He wants us to respond to Him by faith.

The reason God demands faith is that faith is a moral response to His character. Faith gives God the honor that is due His name.

Let me illustrate. A rich person may have many so-called friends, but in the back of his mind he may be wondering, *Do these people love me for who I am or for what I have?* No one wants to be used without being loved.

Likewise, God wants us to love Him not for what He can do, but for who He is. So God refuses to bribe or overwhelm us to make us follow Him.

This helps us understand why Jesus came into the world as He did. He came to reveal the *character* of God, not to display the *grandeur* of God. When He came to this earth, He left all of the splendor and glory and majesty that was inherently His in heaven.

Isaiah said of Jesus in His incarnation, "He hath no form nor comeliness; and when we shall see him, there is no beauty that we should desire him" (Isaiah 53:2).

148

This means that Jesus did not ride out of heaven in a jeweled chariot, wearing regal robes and a diadem on His brow. Rather, He was born in a smelly stable with cow dung on the floor. He was reared in an obscure village as a carpenter's son. He lived a life of poverty and humility.

It is true that He performed miracles, but not to gain followers. His miracles were works of mercy and revelations of truth, not cheap tricks or public-relations stunts. Often He would say after a miracle, "Do not tell anyone about this."

Jesus knew the mind-set of the miracle-mongers, those who wanted Him to give them a sign from heaven so they could believe. These were the ones who followed Him for a while after He had fed the five thousand. But when He preached to them about real commitment, they left Him.

Yet, there were others who loved and followed Jesus sincerely. They did not follow Him primarily for what He did or for what He had, but rather for who He was. They responded by faith to His character and person. A true heart responds to God by faith like a healthy eye responds to light and a healthy ear responds to sound.

The reason, therefore, that God honors faith is that faith honors Him. Faith is a moral response to the character of God. Therefore, above all things it is faith that gives God pleasure.

THROUGH FAITH GOD GIVES US TREASURE

Finally, Hebrews 11:6 tells us that those who believe God find Him to be "a rewarder of them that diligently seek him." Our God longs to show Himself mighty on behalf of people who trust Him. Faith is the key to meeting our needs, whatever they may be. Let me list a few of the needs that faith can supply:

149

Salvation. "Therefore being justified by faith, we have peace with God through our Lord Jesus Christ" (Romans 5:1).

The fullness of the Spirit. ". . . that the blessing of Abraham might come on the Gentiles through Jesus Christ; that we might receive the promise of the Spirit through faith" (Galatians 3:14).

Victory over the world. "This is the victory that overcometh the world, even our faith" (1 John 5:4).

Victory over Satan. "Above all, taking the shield of faith, wherewith ye shall be able to quench all the fiery darts of the wicked" (Ephesians 6:16).

Answered prayer. "Therefore I say unto you, What things soever ye desire, when ye pray, believe that ye receive them, and ye shall have them" (Mark 11:24).

There is an imagined story of a scene in heaven. Some angels approach the throne and say, "Father, there is a mortal on earth asking for a blessing. What is Your pleasure concerning his request?"

The Father asks, "What did he send his faith in?"

The angels answer, "He sent his faith in a thimble."

The Father responds, "Well, fill the thimble with blessings and send it back to him. According to his faith, be it unto him."

Again the angels come and say, "Father, another mortal is asking blessings of Thee."

Again the Father inquires, "And what did he send his faith in?"

The angels respond, "He sent his faith in a huge barrel." With a smile the Father says, "Fill the barrel with blessings and send it back to him. According to his faith, be it unto him."

By faith we give God pleasure, and through faith God gives us treasure.

The Development of Faith

How do we develop this kind of faith? The writer of Hebrews gave us an entire chapter on what others accomplished by faith. Then he spoke to us:

> Wherefore seeing we also are compassed about with so great a cloud of witnesses, let us lay aside every weight, and the sin which doth so easily beset us, and let us run with patience the race that is set before us, looking unto Jesus the author and finisher of our faith; who for the joy that was set before him endured the cross, despising the shame, and is set down at the right hand of the throne of God (Hebrews 12:1–2).

The idea is that these heroes of the faith are now in the heavenly grandstand, while we are in the arena as spiritual athletes running the race of faith.

There are some simple rules given in these verses that tell us how to develop a dynamic faith:

Saturate your heart and mind with the Word of God. Notice the word *wherefore* in verse 1. It refers us to what has already been said—in this case, the entire eleventh chapter of Hebrews, which is devoted to the subject of faith and contains references to almost all of the Old Testament. The point is that the Bible

151

is a book that will develop your faith. Remember Romans 10:17—"So then faith cometh by hearing, and hearing by the word of God."

The Bible may need explaining, but it is first and foremost a book to be believed, not explained. The Bible may be admired, but the promises of the Bible are not so much mottoes to be hung on the wall as they are checks to be cashed at the bank of heaven.

Would you have faith? Love the Bible, study it, memorize it, meditate on it, and obey it, and you will find faith welling up in your heart.

Repent of all known sin. Verse 1 goes on to say, "Let us lay aside every weight, and the sin which doth so easily beset us."

An athlete is foolish if he endeavors to run with excess baggage or anything that would cause him to stumble. The phrase "easily beset" has the meaning of cleverly placing something around an object. Sin can cleverly place itself around us, so as to cause us to stumble in the race of faith.

Remember that unbelief comes from an evil heart. If you are having difficulty believing God, it may be that unconfessed sin is tripping you up.

In the Bible, God often mentions grace and peace together, but grace always comes before peace, for that is God's order. We cannot know His peace until we have experienced His grace.

Likewise, God mentions repentance and faith in that same sequence. If you are having difficulty with faith, you should try repentance. It always comes first. Faith and sin are mutually exclusive.

Use the faith you already have. We are told to "run with patience the race that is set before us." I like the word *run* because it indicates what faith is. Faith is active, not static. It is more than mere belief. Faith is belief with legs on it.

The athlete learns to run by running. Reading books about running is not enough. Lectures on running will not suffice. The athlete must get out on the track and begin to learn. Use the weak faith you have, and it will become stronger faith.

To change the figure of speech, let me remind you that Jesus said faith is like a mustard seed. What's so great about a mustard seed is that though it may be tiny, it has God-given life in it. It is meant not to be treasured but to be planted, so that it will produce so much more.

It has been well said that any fool can count the seeds in an apple, but only God can count the apples in a seed.

Take the faith you have now and put it into action. It will grow as you exercise it. It will produce as you plant it.

Keep your eyes on Jesus. We are told in Hebrews 12:2 to be "looking unto Jesus the author and finisher of our faith." Faith is the by-product of keeping one's eyes upon Jesus.

The word translated "looking" is *aphorao* in the Greek language. It means "to look away from all else unto a certain object." Take your eyes from self, Satan, and circumstances, and turn them to Jesus.

This word also speaks of our dependence and trust on Jesus. Suppose you had a financial need, and a wealthy friend said, "Look to me. I will take care of it." He would not mean that you were simply to look at him, but that you were to depend upon him.

Jesus is worthy of our trust. He alone is the Author and Finisher of our faith. Let His glory and beauty fill your heart right now. Look to Him for every need.

CHAPTER TWELVE

Blessed Assurance

How wonderful it is to be saved, to have the joy of sins forgiven. But there is something even more wonderful—and that is to *know* you are saved.

The assurance of salvation is one of God's greatest gifts to us as the people of His dwelling. Yet, we are told by many Christian leaders and workers who deal with scores of people that the number one question believers have is, "How can I know I'm saved?" The lack of assurance is a great problem among God's people. Living without assurance is like driving with your parking brake on.

But there's no need for this because God's Word says we can know beyond a shadow of a doubt that we are saved. We used to call it a "know-so" salvation, and I think that is still a great description of our salvation.

I was in a hospital once witnessing to a woman. She had not yet given her heart to the Lord Jesus Christ, and the doctor said she did not have long to live. I asked her if she knew the Lord Jesus, and she said no. I asked her, "Would you like to know Christ?"

She answered, "I surely would." So I took God's Word and showed her how she could trust Christ. Then I led her in a prayer, and she invited Jesus Christ into her heart to forgive her sins and to save her once and for all, now and forever.

Some of her loved ones were standing there in the hospital room. I thought they would rejoice, so I turned to her son-in-law and said, "Isn't it wonderful that she's been saved?"

"Oh," he said, "no one can know they're saved."

I replied, "But if a person will trust Christ, they can know they're saved."

He repeated his objection. "No, no one can know they're saved."

This young man was not an unbeliever—that is, he did not repudiate Christianity. He just had a doctrinal stance that would not allow him to accept the fact that a child of God can say, "Praise God, I *know* that I'm saved."

I pointed him to a verse of Scripture I want to consider with you in this chapter, 1 John 5:13. Notice these words very carefully: "These things have I written unto you that believe on the name of the Son of God; that ye may know that ye have eternal life."

Don't miss the point. The apostle John does not say, "that ye may hope that ye have eternal life." Neither does he say that we can only think or surmise or wish that we have eternal life. It is as if God said, "I wrote an entire book of the Bible so that you might *know* you have eternal life." Why did God do this? Because of the vast importance the assurance of salvation has for us.

Settling the Issue of Eternity

Let me show you what I mean. If you do not know you are saved, if you do not know your future—your eternal destiny— you had better get it settled. This is an all-important issue. We are not talking about denominational preference. We are not talking about whether you like the choir music or not. We are talking about eternity.

Where you will spend eternity is so vitally important that I do not want you to have any doubt at all about your destiny. Actually, I have two purposes in this chapter. I want to, as Vance Havner used to say, "comfort the afflicted and afflict the comfortable."

That is, if you are genuinely saved, I pray that by the time you finish reading this chapter you will *know* you are saved. But if you are not saved and are merely clinging to some experience that happened thirty years ago and have no spiritual reality in the present, then you need to feel uncomfortable about the issue of your salvation.

As we will see later on in this chapter, the Bible never points one back to a past experience for the assurance of his salvation. Belief and assurance are always in the present tense.

Before we go any further, I want to set 1 John 5:13 in its larger context:

Who is he that overcometh the world, but he that believeth that Jesus is the Son of God? This is he that came by water and blood, even Jesus Christ; not by water only, but by water and blood. And it is the Spirit that beareth witness, because the Spirit is truth. For there are three that bear record in heaven, the Father, the Word, and the Holy Ghost: and these three are one. And there are three that bear witness in earth, the Spirit, and the water, and the blood: and these three agree in one. If we receive the witness of men, the witness of God is greater: for this is the witness of God which he hath testified of his Son. He that believeth on the Son of God hath the witness in himself: he that believeth not God hath made him a liar; because he believeth not the record that God gave of his Son. And this is the record, that God hath given to us eternal life, and this life is in his Son. He that hath the Son hath life; and he that hath not the Son of God hath not life. These things have I written unto you that believe on the name of the Son of God; that ye may know that ye have eternal life, and that ye may believe on the name of the Son of God (vv. 5–13).

The word *know* means "absolute assurance." If verse 13 means anything, it means you can know you are saved. It is possible to be saved and know it, but we have to recognize that it is also possible to be saved and doubt it. If doubt were not possible, John would not have needed to assure us that we can have a know-so salvation. He is writing to people who might have doubt in order that they might have assurance.

Can a person be saved and have doubts? Yes. Is doubt good? No. Doubt is to your spirit what pain is to your body. Pain is a warning, a signal that something is wrong. If you have doubts, and if you truly are a born-again child of God, those doubts are a signal that something is amiss.

All Christians have doubts from time to time. A woman once told Dwight L. Moody she had been saved for twenty-five years and never had a doubt.

Moody replied, "I doubt you're saved."

What did Moody mean by that? Well, it would be like your saying to me, "Adrian, I've been married twenty-five years and have never had an argument with my spouse."

I would say to you, "I doubt you're married."

I am not saying that arguing with your spouse is good—not at all. And I am not saying that doubting your Lord is good—not at all. There is no need to be a doubting Christian when you can be a shouting Christian. I want to help you remove doubt and have the certainty, the assurance, of your salvation.

As a matter of fact, if you will read through the book of 1 John and circle the word *know*, you will be amazed at how many times the apostle uses that word. It is an epistle of assurance.

How to Know You're Saved

Let me tell you how I know that Adrian Rogers knows he is saved. It is not because of any confidence I have in myself, but I do know I am saved, and I bless God that I know I am saved. I want to show you from God's Word how you can have that same assurance.

A PRESENT FAITH IN THE SON OF GOD

If I would have the assurance of my salvation, there must be a present, "right-now" faith in Jesus.

The key here is in 1 John 5:10: "He that believeth on the Son of God hath the witness in himself." Then verse 13: "These things have I written unto you that believe on the name of the Son of God."

The word I want to underline is *believe*, because in the Bible the words *believe* and *commit* are the same word. You can see this in John 2:23–24, where the Bible says concerning Jesus, "Many believed in his name, when they saw the miracles which he did. But Jesus did not commit himself unto them."

The people said they believed in Jesus, but He did not believe in them. He knew they were just miracle-mongers, not true believers. You see, true biblical faith is not just an intellectual exercise. You do not believe *about* Jesus—you believe *in* Jesus. You commit yourself to Him.

Let me illustrate. Whenever I would board an airplane, I would commit myself to it. I did not just believe the airplane could fly. I did not just believe there was a good pilot at the controls. I would get on that airplane and commit myself to it.

I want you to notice something very important here that has a great deal to do with the assurance of your salvation. The Bible does not say, "He that has believed," but "He that believes." The Bible does not speak of faith in the past tense. It is always present tense.

Have you ever asked someone, "Are you saved?"

"Yes, I'm saved," is the answer.

"Tell me about it."

"Well, I remember back when I was a nine-year-old child, I walked down the aisle and gave my hand to my pastor and my heart to Jesus Christ. I may not be living for God right now, I'll admit, but I know I'm saved because I remember what I did when I was nine. I remember believing on Jesus Christ."

It may surprise you to know that the Bible never encourages you to use an experience as proof of your salvation. The Bible never points back to some time when you believed on Jesus Christ.

I hear people say, "If you cannot name the time and place when you received Christ, you're not saved." That sounds good, but there's just one thing wrong with it—you won't find it in the Bible. The Bible never says you can know you are saved by what you remember in the past. Faith is always present tense.

If you want to know whether you are saved, ask yourself if you are believing in Jesus Christ right now. Are you committed to Him? Are you trusting Him today?

Please do not misunderstand. I am not saying the time you received Christ is not important. Unless you did that, you are not saved. Praise God for the day and the hour of your salvation. But that is not where assurance comes from. The acid test is, are you now believing in Jesus Christ? Are you trusting in Him at this moment with all of your heart and soul?

When I fly from Memphis to Dallas, for example, it's not important that I recall the moment we crossed the Texas state line. The proof that we flew into Texas is that I am now on the ground at DFW airport. Those who came to Texas by car may know when they crossed the state line, but the proof that I crossed the state line is that I am now sitting at the airport in Dallas.

Correspondingly, the assurance that I am saved comes not from the fact that I did trust Christ, but that I am now trusting Christ. I am now at this very moment trusting my eternal destiny to the One Who gave all for me.

Why should you not have this blessed assurance? Does the claim for assurance sound arrogant? It is not arrogance or self-confidence but rather God-confidence that brings assurance. True assurance is in the full and finished work of Calvary. If even the smallest part depends upon me, I have no ground for assurance.

A youngster once came forward at church to present himself as a candidate for baptism. As the leaders questioned him about his salvation to make sure he understood what it meant to trust Christ, the boy assured them he was saved, explaining, "I did my part, and God did His part."

"What do you mean by that?" one questioned.

"I did the sinning, and God did the saving," he replied.

A BASIS FOR MY BELIEF

A second necessity if I am to have the assurance of my salvation is this: there must be a firm basis for my belief. If indeed I must be trusting Christ now, how do I know the object of my faith is reliable and authentic?

What is it that Christians believe? And why do we believe? Are we just gullible? Are we believing in fairy tales, or is there a basis for our belief? Why do we believe what we believe? The apostle John gives us three wonderful bases or roots for our belief:

The Work of Christ

You will find this great assurance in 1 John 5:6: "This is he that came by water and blood, even Jesus Christ; not by water only, but by water and blood." The Bible tells us that when the Lord Jesus Christ was crucified they ran a spear into His side, and out came water and blood (John 19:33–34). Jesus died the excruciating, painful death of crucifixion, and out of His wounded side flowed water and blood.

We are saved by blood and sanctified by water. When a person entered the Old Testament tabernacle—which we have already seen was a picture of the presence of God (that is, the Lord Jesus Christ)—the first thing he encountered was the bronze altar upon which the bloody sacrifices were made. Then there was a laver or great basin that the priest would wash in. So there was first the blood, and then the water.

That was all a picture of the work of Christ on the cross. The Bible says He came by the saving blood and the sanctifying water. His blood forgives us, and the sanctifying water keeps us clean. We sing about it all the time:

Let the water and the blood,
From thy wounded side which flowed,
Be of sin the double cure,
Save from wrath and make me pure.[1]

One way you can know you are saved is that Jesus Christ, the Son of God, died to purchase your salvation. That is a historical fact. That is the saving work of Christ. All assurance must rest on that!

The Witness of the Spirit

Here is another way we can know we are saved. In 1 John 5:6b–8, John says:

> It is the Spirit that beareth witness, because the Spirit is truth. For there are three that bear record in heaven, the Father, the Word, and the Holy Ghost: and these three are one. And there are three that bear witness in earth, the Spirit, and the water, and the blood: and these three agree in one.

In other words, the Holy Spirit takes the water and the blood and applies them to our hearts.

Now, notice the argument in verse 9: "If we receive the witness of men, the witness of God is greater: for this is the witness of God which he hath testified of his Son." The fact that Jesus Christ died on the cross, that He came by water and blood, is established in history.

But how is that made real to us? How do we know there was a man named Jesus Christ who was the sinless Son of God? How do we know that God sent Him and that He actually

163

died on that cross and took our sin upon Himself? We do not have to depend upon somebody's argument because the Holy Spirit of God is here to make it all real in our hearts.

God gave us the work of Christ. But then to make the work of Christ (the water and the blood) real to us, He gave us the Spirit.

Here in 1 John 5:9 the word *If* may be translated "since"— "Since we receive the witness of men . . ." All of us believe the witness of men. Every time I fly I receive the witness of an airline about a person I have never met before—the pilot. I don't ask to see his credentials. That airline has its stamp of approval on the pilot; so I just get on the plane and never think twice about it. You do too, I am sure.

We do the same thing when we eat in a restaurant. How do you know the food is not poisoned? You exercise faith in the people who prepared it. Again, your doctor writes you a prescription you can't even read. You carry it down to the drugstore, your pharmacist fills it, and you go home and take that medicine, the name of which you cannot pronounce and which was given to you by a man you hardly know. Why? Because we receive the witness of men.

John's argument is that we have the work of Christ and the witness of the Spirit, which are far greater and far more reliable than the witness of men. Don't tell me you can't believe. I do not believe that you can't believe. Do you know why? Because if you want to believe, the Holy Spirit will help you. No one can say, "I can't believe." God eliminates that excuse because people who receive the witness of men can receive the witness of God through the Holy Spirit.

I can preach truth, but only the Holy Spirit can impart truth. This is why I soak every sermon in prayer before I preach it. The apostles said, "We are his witnesses of these things; and so is also the Holy Ghost, whom God hath given to them that obey him" (Acts 5:32). First of all, the Holy Spirit witnesses to us.

Then He witnesses in us, according to 1 John 5:10. Before I got saved, the Spirit witnessed to me. He told me that what Jesus Christ did is true. And now He witnesses in me. I have the witness in myself.

Suppose I am enjoying a piece of apple pie. You come to me and say, "There is no such thing as apple pie. I don't believe in apple pie. And if there is apple pie, it is no good."

Well, I want to tell you, in spite of all your arguments, I have the witness within me! A Christian with a testimony is never at the mercy of an unbeliever with an argument because the Christian has the witness in himself.

I must be careful here. The witness of the Spirit is not some emotion. It is not feeling warm around the heart or wet around the lashes. It is deeper than our emotions. Our emotions are the shallowest part of our nature. Salvation is the deepest work of God. God does not do His deepest work in the shallowest part. The witness of the Spirit, therefore, is not emotion, but rather God the Holy Spirit in His own way whispering to me that I belong to Jesus.

This always reminds me of a delightful incident that once happened to a good friend of mine. He and his wife were driving through the Smoky Mountains, enjoying the scenery. It began to get dark, and he was low on gas. His wife asked him if they shouldn't be getting gas somewhere, but he assured her they had enough for now.

Well, as these things often happen, he kept driving, thinking that surely he would find a gas station soon. But there were no stations, and by now he was in trouble. He prayed, "Lord, help me find a gas station." He knew that if he didn't, there would be murder in the mountains!

He came around a turn and saw a country gas station with one of those old glass pumps. My friend knocked on the door, and an old mountaineer came out to pump the gas. His head was down as he kept his eye on the nozzle of that ancient pump.

My friend was so relieved that he took a deep breath of mountain air and with a smile said, "It's great to be alive."

The old mountaineer never lifted his head but just replied, "I wouldn't know. I've never been no other way."

Well, my friend, I can tell you I have been some other way. I was dead in my sin, and it's great to be alive in Christ! I have the witness of the Spirit on the inside.

The Word of the Father

The Word of the Father is a third basis for my belief. It is "the record that God gave of His Son" (1 John 5:10b).

What is this "record"? It is God's Word, the Bible, which tells us that we have eternal life in the Lord Jesus Christ. Verse 12 makes this so plain. If you have the Son, you have life. That brings us back to verse 13, which is our spiritual birth certificate.

Here is the basis of our belief, the reason for our certainty. We are not just gullible fools. Jesus Christ died. He came by water and blood. The Holy Spirit of God says, "Yes, this is true. It's all attested by the Word of God."

To doubt the Bible is to call God a liar (v. 10). Someone may say, "Well, I'm trying to believe." Don't pride yourself in that.

Suppose I told you something, and you said, "Adrian, I'm trying to believe you."

I reply, "It's true."

"Well, I'm trying to believe you."

What you mean is, you are not certain whether I am telling the truth or not. But if you do not believe me, you have just cut the taproot of my character. If you refuse to believe God, you have made Him a liar. Either the Bible is His Word or it is not His Word. This is the root of our belief: the work of Christ, the witness of the Spirit, and the Word of the Father.

Thank God, we are not just gullible people. Our faith is not autosuggestion. There's a reason for believing. We have the inerrant, infallible Word of God. We do not have to surmise on that. It has been tested through the ages.

It's so good to have the written Word rather than just emotions. Suppose I am in a courtroom, and the judge says to me, "Mr. Rogers, are you married?"

I say, "Yes, I am."

"Can you prove you're married?"

"Yes, I can, Your Honor. I was there in the church, and I saw Joyce coming down the aisle. My heart got all twitterpated, and I was so happy. Your Honor, it's the most wonderful feeling in the world to be married."

What will the judge say? "I'm happy you feel that way. But your emotions are not admissible as evidence in this court. Do you have any proof of your marriage?"

So I go down to the courthouse and get my marriage license, all properly signed and recorded, and I bring it to the judge. He says, "Okay, that's better."

I am glad I have something better than my emotions to assure me of my salvation. I have the Word of God.

A BELIEF THAT WILL SHOW IN BEHAVIOR

If I am to have the assurance of my salvation, I must first have a present belief in the Son of God. Second, there must be a basis for my belief. And third, what I believe must show in my behavior.

So it is fitting to ask, what has my salvation done in me? The English word *believe* comes from the two words "by live." What we truly believe, we live by. Is this all just an exercise in philosophy? Or has there been a change in my life? How do I know God is at home in my heart?

John is very, very practical here. He gives us theological truths, the bases of our belief. Then he shows us how these truths ought to show up in our behavior by giving us some primary tests. If you want to examine your heart and life, read on and see if you measure up.

The Commandment Test

This is the issue of who is Lord of your house. If you are a genuine Christian, then your house, your temple, is under new management:

> And hereby we do know that we know him, if we keep his commandments. He that saith, I know him, and keepeth not his commandments, is a liar, and the truth is not in him. But whoso keepeth his word, in him verily is the love of God perfected: hereby know we that we are in him. He that saith he abideth in him ought himself so to walk, even as he walked (1 John 2:3–6).

John says your walk must match your talk or you are lying about your salvation. This is what I call afflicting the comfortable. If you are a genuine, born-again child of God, that is going to show in your life. You are going to be keeping the commandments of God. Now, you do not keep the commandments of God in order to be saved. You keep the commandments of God *because* you are saved.

This brings a problem, because not one of us has always kept all of God's commandments. Yet, the Bible says this is the way we can know that we are in Christ.

Sounds kind of frightening, doesn't it? But remember, John wants to give us assurance of our salvation, not send us out on a futile quest for perfection. It's all wrapped up in that word *keep*. This is a mariner's word, a sailor's word.

In that day, sailors did not sail by all of the modern instruments of navigation. They set their course by the stars. A sailor navigating by the stars was said to be "keeping" the stars. His intention was to sail by the stars. That was his desire and goal.

In the same way, God says we are to "keep" His commandments. The desire, the goal, the guide for our lives is to be the Word of God, the commandments of Jesus Christ. You cannot say you have been saved if your desire is not to live by the Word of God. You may get blown off course, or there may be a time when you will get confused. But the aim, the goal, of your life should be to keep the commandments of God. We are not saved by faith and works but by faith that works (James 2:22–26).

Ever since I gave my heart to Jesus, there has been a divine, deep, and radical change in me and a burning desire to live for God. Is that true in you? If not, you do not need assurance of your salvation. You need to get saved.

The question is not whether we ever sin. The difference is, before I got saved I was running to sin. Now I am running *from* it. The desire of my heart is to live by the Word of God. If that's not the desire of your heart, you had better go back and check up on your salvation again.

This is the commandment test. If you can willfully and knowingly sin against the will of God with no conviction, no compunction, and no remorse, you need to get saved. Some may say, "I professed Christ once and was saved. I know I'm just an old backslider now, but I'm still saved and going to heaven."

Think again, my friend. If you can live sinfully—high, wide, and handsome—and it doesn't break your heart, if there is no conviction, no remorse over sin, you do not know the God of the Bible. Is Jesus the Lord of your house?

The Companion Test

Another test by which we can judge the fruit of our behavior is the companion test. "We know that we have passed from death unto life, because we love the brethren" (1 John 3:14).

When I am saved, I want to be *right* with my brother, and I want to *be* with my brother. Someone will say, "Well, I'm saved, but I have no desire to go to church. I have no use for the people of God." However, if you have no desire to be with the saints down here, you have little hope of being with them up there. John says if you love Jesus—if He is not only the *Lord* of your house but the *love* of your house—you are going to love what Jesus loves. And Jesus loves the church.

Did you know that the word *saint* is seldom used in the Bible? It's almost always *saints*, plural—your brothers and sisters in Christ. Jesus takes this very seriously. When you despise the church, you despise Jesus. When Paul was on his way to Damascus to persecute Christians, Jesus asked him, "Saul, Saul, why persecutest thou me?" (Acts 9:4).

Paul could have said, "Whoever you are, I am not persecuting you. I am persecuting the church." But the inference is obvious: to persecute the church is to persecute Jesus. And to love the church is to love Jesus.

Billy Sunday used to say, "It's true that going to church will not make you a Christian, any more than going into a garage will make you an automobile." But when you realize you have been bought by the blood of Christ, when the Spirit of God comes to indwell you and you receive a new nature, when your desire is to keep God's commandments, then you are going to love the people of God. Is your house a headquarters for hate, or is Jesus who indwells you manifesting His love for the church?

Remember that keeping the commandments and loving our brothers do not save us, but they are evidences of our faith. They are evidences, not requirements, and yet they are part of the normal Christian's life. If they are not present, either you are lost or you are terribly backslidden and have no reason for assurance.

If you have genuine doubt about whether you are saved, ask God now to come into your heart and save you. Trust Him, and He will do it.

If that doesn't give you assurance, your problem may be somewhere else. There may be a broken relationship or a broken commandment that must be put right. May God give you a blessed assurance as Christ dwells in your heart by faith.

CHAPTER THIRTEEN

God's House Is Not a Hotel

I suggested in chapter 12 that as wonderful as it is to be saved, it is even more wonderful to *know* that you are saved.

But did you know there is something more wonderful still? It is even more wonderful to know that you are saved *forever*. This is the security of the believer. Assurance tells me how to know I have salvation, security tells me that once I have it, I can never lose it.

Jesus has made known to us a very thrilling truth, which is this: when God moves into the human heart, He moves in to stay. Jesus said of the Holy Spirit, "I will pray the Father, and he shall give you another Comforter, that he may abide with you for ever" (John 14:16).

The word *abide* may be translated "continue," "dwell," "endure," "remain," or "stand." God has come to settle down in us. My friend Ron Dunn put it well when he said, "My heart is not a hotel with check-out time at twelve noon on Sunday."

God's abiding presence is what theologians call the eternal security of the believer. This is a truth that ought to bring strength and joy to your heart, and I cannot think of a better

173

note on which to conclude our study of the indwelling presence of Christ.

When I speak of His abiding presence—the eternal security of the believer in Christ—I want to make something clear. I am not speaking about the security of those who merely profess to be saved. There are many professors of salvation who are not possessors of salvation. Outwardly they may look, act, and talk like Christians, but they have never been redeemed.

Jesus spoke an emphatic word of warning concerning these pretenders who have never been born again: "Many will say to me in that day, Lord, Lord, have we not prophesied in thy name? and in thy name have cast out devils? and in thy name done many wonderful works? And then will I profess unto them, I never knew you: depart from me, ye that work iniquity" (Matthew 7:22–23).

Note the phrase that Jesus used: "I never knew you." We have all seen people who make a false start and then fall away and even deny the faith they once professed. They did not lose their salvation because they never had it.

Jesus said, "I never knew you." I do not know who first coined this little statement, but it says it well: "The faith that fizzles before the finish had a flaw from the first."

I call these people who start out fine and then fade away "Alka-Seltzer Christians." You drop them in water, they fizzle a little bit, but then they disappear.

The apostle John made reference to people like this when he said, "They went out from us, but they were not of us; for if they had been of us, they would no doubt have continued with us: but they went out, that they might be made manifest that they were not all of us" (1 John 2:19). Notice that they had never been added to the Body of Christ through the new birth.

But those who are truly saved have God's promise that He will never leave them. Think with me about seven wonderful reasons why someone who has been made a partaker of the divine nature can never ever again be a lost soul.

The Perseverance of the Spirit

This is a wonderful truth expressed by the apostle Paul: "Being confident of this very thing, that he which hath begun a good work in you will perform it until the day of Jesus Christ" (Philippians 1:6).

Who is it that has begun this "good work" in us, and who is going to carry it on to completion? The Holy Spirit, of course. And this verse says that what He has begun, He will finish.

Have you ever started something you couldn't finish? I think this is a trait common to human nature. I heard of a youngster named Billy who said to his dad, "Daddy, Jimmy says that his dad has a list of men he can whip, and your name is the first one on the list."

So Billy's daddy went and confronted Jimmy's daddy. "My son says you have a list of men you can whip, and my name is first on the list. Is that right?"

"Yes, that's right."

"Well, you can't do it! What are you going to do about that?" Billy's dad said.

"Then I guess I'll just have to take your name off the list," said Jimmy's dad.

It is not a trait of omnipotence, however, to start things that it cannot finish. When God saved us, our names were recorded in heaven; and God will never take our names off the list because He was not able to finish what He began.

Just think what the Holy Spirit does in our salvation. He is the *Convicter*, the One Who shows us our sins and convinces us of our guilt.

He is also the *Converter*, the One Who works the marvelous work of grace in our hearts so that we are "born of the Spirit" (John 3:8).

And since the Spirit is the Convicter and the Converter, He is also the *Completer*. He will finish what He has begun. He will not abandon you as some half-completed relic.

The Perfection of the Sacrifice

When Jesus died on the cross, He offered a perfect sacrifice that made us perfect forever. "For by one offering he hath perfected for ever them that are sanctified" (Hebrews 10:14).

In Old Testament times, when a sacrifice for sin was made, it was never perfect or complete. Those priests had to come time and again with bloody sacrifices to those smoking altars because those sacrifices were only shadows and prophecies of that perfect sacrifice to come.

> For the law having a shadow of good things to come, and not the very image of the things, can never with those sacrifices which they offered year by year continually make the comers thereunto perfect. For then would they not have ceased to be offered? because that the worshippers once purged should have had no more conscience of sins. But in those sacrifices there is a remembrance again made of sins every year. For it is not possible that the blood of bulls and of goats should take away sins (Hebrews 10:1–4).

All those sacrifices did was to roll the sins of the people forward one more year. But when Jesus shed His rich, royal blood on that cross, everything was paid in full. And because of that sacrifice, we are "perfected for ever." We don't get just a fresh start or a new chance but an eternal perfection.

Think with me for a moment. If it were possible for one to lose his salvation (which, of course, it isn't), then for that person to be saved a second time Jesus would have to die a second time. But what He did at Calvary was good for eternal salvation. It was one offering, and it was forever.

This is why if you search the Scriptures through, you will never find mention of anyone ever being saved twice. Our salvation is once for all, and if it is not "once saved, always saved," it would have to be "twice lost, always lost." How I thank God that when Jesus died for me, He perfected me forever.

The Position of the Saved

When we are saved, not only does Christ come to live in us, but we also take our position in Him. "Therefore if any man be in Christ, he is a new creature: old things are passed away; behold, all things are become new" (2 Corinthians 5:17).

This verse clearly states our position "in Christ." That means, among other things, that we are actually a part of His mystical body.

For me ever to be separated from Him and be eternally lost would also mean that a part of Jesus was eternally lost. I have been made a part of His very body. Christ is the invisible part of the visible Christian. And a Christian is the visible part of the invisible Christ. We are in Him, and He is in us.

Peter showed us that our position in Christ is illustrated by Noah's position in the ark (see 1 Peter 3:18–22). When that ark was finished, a perfect way of escape from the wrath of God had been provided. That's because the ark was covered "within and without with pitch" (Genesis 6:14). The Hebrew word for *pitch* is exactly the same word that is translated elsewhere as "atonement." Thank God for the atonement that keeps the waters of God's wrath from reaching His rescued ones!

Noah was not told to place pegs on the outside of the ark so he could hold on. That would have been ridiculous, and yet this is the kind of salvation some people think they have. They feel they will get to heaven if they can just hold out faithful to the end. But people who believe this have forgotten who is holding whom (John 10:28–29).

Imagine this scene: Noah is holding on to a slimy peg on the outside of the ark. His knuckles have turned white. He shouts above the roar of the storm to Mrs. Noah, "Honey, please pray for me that I'll hold out faithful to the end." Poor old Noah never would have made it.

Thank God it was not that way at all. God said to Noah, "Come thou and all thy house into the ark" (Genesis 7:1). God was already inside the ark inviting Noah to come in with Him! It was then that God shut and sealed the door.

Not only did God shut the water out, but at the same time He closed Noah in with Himself. Noah was as safe as the ark itself was safe because he was in the ark. We are likewise in Christ. We will go down only if He goes down.

It seems to me that all Christians believe in some kind of security. Most believe their security will begin when they get to heaven. They picture themselves stepping over the threshold of the celestial city, heaving a sigh of relief, and saying, "I made it! I'm safe!"

But wait a moment! No one is safe just because he is in heaven. The Scripture teaches that the glorious angels fell from heaven. Security is not in a place but in a Person! His name is Jesus; He is our ark of safety.

You see, we have something that even angels do not have. I would rather be a saved sinner than an innocent angel. We are safe in Christ, and that is the only safety we have or need.

The Predestination of the Saint

> And we know that all things work together for good to them that love God, to them who are the called according to his purpose. For whom he did foreknow, he also did predestinate to be conformed to the image of his Son, that he might be the firstborn among many brethren. Moreover whom he did predestinate, them he also called: and whom he called, them he also justified: and whom he justified, them he also glorified (Romans 8:28–30).

The child of God, according to this Scripture, has been foreknown in the mind of God since before the foundation of the world. Theologians have debated and dialogued about predestination for ages, and there have been some farfetched interpretations. Some feel that every event of our lives has been minutely programmed ahead of time, and there is nothing that we can do to change it.

The story is told of a little old lady who fell down the cellar stairs, got up, brushed herself off, and said, "I'm glad that's over with."

I don't believe in that kind of predestination. But I do believe that God will carry out His great, eternal purposes in the lives of every man and woman, boy, and girl who places his or her faith in Jesus Christ.

Whenever I fly from one city to another, my actions on the airplane are more or less of my own choosing. Yet the plane is headed to a predetermined destination. Humanly speaking, it is predestined to arrive in a certain city.

Now the airlines cannot always make it to their predetermined destinations. But what God predestines, He fulfills. I am predestined to be "conformed to the image of his Son," and all hell cannot stop it.

As a matter of fact, verse 30 speaks of me as having already been glorified. The verb is in the past tense. I do not have to wait until I die to see whether I am going to heaven.

In the council halls of eternity, I have already been glorified. In the heart and mind of God, it is already done. What has been settled in eternity cannot be undone in time; what has been decreed by heaven cannot be annulled by hell. Anyone predestined to be conformed to the image of God's Son is as secure as he could possibly be.

The Present Tense of Salvation

Eternal life means life that will never end. The believer has eternal life; he has life that is endless.

Consider this carefully. Eternal life does not begin for the Christian when he dies; it begins when he believes. "Verily, verily, I say unto you, He that heareth my word, and believeth on him that sent me, hath everlasting life, and shall not come into condemnation; but is passed from death unto life" (John 5:24).

This verse clearly tells me that I now have eternal life. If this is true, how could I ever cease to exist with God? How could I ever again be a lost soul?

If a man were a Christian for ten years and then became lost, all he would have had was "ten-year life." Whatever you have, if you ever lose it, it is not eternal. Thank God that the believer "is passed from death unto life," and the life he now has is "everlasting."

The Prayers of the Savior

Another reason for our security in the Lord Jesus Christ is the intercession of our dear Savior. The finished work of Jesus was His atonement on the cross. As He was dying in agony and blood, these words burst from His bruised lips: "It is finished" (John 19:30). And thank God it was! That was the perfect sacrifice of which we have already spoken.

But not only is there the finished work of the Savior—there is also His *unfinished* work. "Wherefore he is able also to save them to the uttermost that come unto God by him, seeing he ever liveth to make intercession for them" (Hebrews 7:25).

Christ is ever-living and ever-interceding. How He intercedes and prays for His own is seen in His great, high-priestly prayer in John 17. Notice the ones for whom Jesus is interceding: "I pray for them: I pray not for the world, but for them which thou hast given me; for they are thine" (v. 9). It is clear that He is praying for His own—the saints, His born-again ones.

And what is He praying for them? "I pray not that thou shouldest take them out of the world, but that thou shouldest keep them from the evil" (v. 15). He is praying for their keeping, for their eternal security.

We know that when Jesus prayed for their security, He was heard, for Jesus Himself said, "thou hearest me always" (John 11:42). Jesus never prayed a prayer that was not answered. So that clearly means that those for whom He has prayed will be securely kept.

Now here is the exciting part for us. He was not just praying for those early disciples—Peter, James, and John and their contemporaries. By faith, Jesus looked down through the tunnel of time and prayed for you and for me also: "Neither pray I for these alone, but for them also which shall believe on me through their word" (v. 20). He might as well have inserted our names.

The intercessory work of Jesus is illustrated in the life of Peter. He was weak in the flesh, but he had a heart full of faith in Christ. Jesus, knowing Peter's weakness, predicted that he would deny Him three times.

But here is the comforting part. Jesus also said, "But I have prayed for thee, that thy faith fail not" (Luke 22:32). Though Peter stumbled, he did not utterly fall. He was weak, but Jesus had prayed for him; so his faith did not fail. The cowardly Peter became the apostle of Pentecost.

I might note here that Jesus never prayed such prayers for Judas. Peter had placed his faith in Christ, but Judas had never done so: "'But there are some of you that believe not.' For Jesus knew from the beginning who they were that believed not, and who should betray him" (John 6:64). "He spake of Judas Iscariot the son of Simon: for he it was that should betray him, being one of the twelve" (v. 71).

Judas never lost his salvation, for he had no salvation to lose. He never was a believer. That was the fundamental difference between Judas and Peter.

Judas may have looked better outwardly, but Peter had a heart of faith. And because he did, Jesus interceded for him. People like us, weak as we are, have a Savior who ever lives to make intercession for us. What a security we have.

The Power of God's Sovereignty

> Blessed be the God and Father of our Lord Jesus Christ, which according to his abundant mercy hath begotten us again unto a lively hope by the resurrection of Jesus Christ from the dead, to an inheritance incorruptible, and undefiled, and that fadeth not away, reserved in heaven for you, who are kept by the power of God through faith unto salvation ready to be revealed in the last time (1 Peter 1:3–5).

We are kept by the power of God! What a comforting thought. Is there a loving parent anywhere who would not preserve his children from death or disaster if it were in his or her power to do so?

Yet, as parents we often fail because we do not have the power to perform our heart's desire. This is never true, however, with Almighty God. He has the power to keep His children.

In Romans 8, we have already seen that we are predestined for glory. But that great chapter goes on to teach that because we are *predestined* for glory, we are also preserved for glory.

No Fault Can Defile Us

I know that I am weak, but, thank God, in spite of my weakness and sin there is no one who can condemn me. In the face of the accuser comes the perfect answer—the upraised and pierced hand of my Intercessor.

> Who shall lay any thing to the charge of God's elect? It is God that justifieth. Who is he that condemneth? It is Christ that died, yea rather, that is risen again, who is even at the right hand of God, who also maketh intercession for us (Romans 8:33–34).

No Foe Can Destroy Us

All the enemies of the Christian do not separate him from the Lord, but only draw him all the closer.

> For I am persuaded, that neither death, nor life, nor angels, nor principalities, nor powers, nor things present, nor things to come, nor height, nor depth, nor any other creature, shall be able to separate us from the love of God, which is in Christ Jesus our Lord (Romans 8:38–39).

Romans 8 begins with *no condemnation* and ends with *no separation.* How I long that God's people would understand what a wonderful salvation they have in the Lord Jesus Christ. He moves into our hearts to stay.

I am aware that some call this teaching of the security of the believer a dangerous doctrine. But if it is true, it cannot possibly be dangerous. The reasoning of those who believe that there is a danger in teaching security is this: they fear that a Christian who feels he is secure will relax, let his guard down, and enter into a sinful lifestyle.

Sometimes it is explained like this: "If I believed in eternal security, then I would get saved and sin all I want to, since nothing I do could ever cause me to lose my salvation."

There are two fatal flaws in this line of reasoning. The first is that when a person says he wants to characteristically or habitually sin, he is giving evidence that he has never been saved at all.

Then again, there is a sense in which I sin all I want to. As a matter of fact, I sin more than I want to because I don't want to. God knows how often I fail. But from the time I said an everlasting yes to Jesus until this moment there has been in my heart a desire to live a holy life.

If you still want to sin, you need a new birth. And with the new birth, you will get a new "want."

Second, we need not think that security is a license to sin with impunity. The heavenly Father will surely chastise His children if they are disobedient. "For whom the Lord loveth he chasteneth, and scourgeth every son whom he receiveth. If ye endure chastening, God dealeth with you as with sons; for what son is he whom the father chasteneth not?" (Hebrews 12:6–7).

That chastisement may take many forms. It may be the sense of broken fellowship or perhaps the loss of joy. It may mean that our prayers do not get through. It may mean a loss of health or prosperity. But even in all of this, the Father is dealing with us in love. It is comforting to know that He loves us enough to chastise us.

It is also so very comforting to know that God has promised, "I will never leave thee, nor forsake thee" (Hebrews 13:5). If you are a believer in Jesus Christ, you do not have to hold on for dear life to Him. He is holding on to you!

Hear His wonderful promise to you: "I give unto [your name] eternal life; and [your name] shall never perish, neither shall any man pluck [your name] out of my hand. My Father, which gave [your name] me, is greater than all; and no man is able to pluck [your name] out of my Father's hand" (John 10:28–29).

Dear reader, this is all the security you will ever need, both now and forever. Amen!

Notes

CHAPTER ONE: WHERE ON EARTH DOES GOD LIVE?
1. Merrill F. Unger, *Unger's Bible Dictionary* (Chicago: Moody Press, 1986), 1065.
2. *Ibid.*, 1076.
3. Ian Thomas, *The Saving Life of Christ* (Grand Rapids, Mich.: Zondervan Publishing House, 1961), 19.

CHAPTER TWO: SUPERNATURALLY NATURAL, NATURALLY SUPERNATURAL
1. William Hendriksen, *Exposition of Colossians and Philemon, New Testament Commentary* (Grand Rapids, Mich.: Baker Book House, 1964), 164.
2. F. F. Bruce, *Ephesians and Colossians, The New International Commentary on the New Testament* (Grand Rapids, Mich.: Eerdmans, 1979), 285.

CHAPTER FOUR: WHEN GLORY FILLS THE HOUSE
1. Hymnary.org "Rescue the Perishing," words by Fanny J. Crosby, 1869. Music by William H. Doane, 1870. Public domain. http://www.hymnary.org/text/rescue_the_perishing_care_for_the_dying
2. "Colorful Sayings from Colorful Moody," *Christian History*, Issue 25 (Vol. 9, No. 1), 9.
3. Hymnary.org "Never Alone," by Ludie D. Pickett, 1897. Public domain. http://www.hymnary.org/text/ive_seen_the_lightning_flashing

CHAPTER SEVEN: LIKE A RIVER GLORIOUS
1. Robert W. Yarbrough, *John: Everyman's Bible Commentary* (Chicago: Moody Press, 1991), 83.
2. Robert Burns, ed. Charles W. Eliot, *The Poems and Songs of Robert Burns*, Vol. 6 (New York: P. F. Collier & Son, 1909–14), http://www.bartleby.com/6/355.html

3. Vance Havner, *Pepper 'n Salt* (Grand Rapids: Fleming H. Revell Company, 1966), http://vancehavner.com/?p=797
4. *Moody Monthly*, April 1975, 61.
5. Hymnary.org "Like a River Glorious," words by Frances Ridley Havergal, 1874. Music by James Mountain, 1876. Public domain. http://www.hymnary.org/text/like_a_river_glorious

CHAPTER EIGHT: KEEPING YOUR HOUSE CLEAN
1. Hymnary.org, "Count Your Blessings," words by Johnson Oatman, Jr., 1897. Music by Edwin O. Excell, 1897. Public domain. http://www.hymnary.org/text/when_upon_lifes_billows_you_are_tempest

CHAPTER NINE: KEEPING YOUR DOORS LOCKED
1. Debora Tkac, ed., *The Doctor's Book of Home Remedies* (Emmaus, Penn.: Rodale Press, 1991), 645.

CHAPTER TEN: A HOUSE OF PRAYER—NOT A DEN OF THIEVES
1. Alfred Plummer, *The Gospel According to St. Matthew* (Minneapolis: James Family Publishers, n.d.), 97.

CHAPTER TWELVE: BLESSED ASSURANCE
1. Hymnary.org, "Rock of Ages," words by Augustus M. Toplady, 1775, 1776. Music by Thomas Hastings, 1832. Public domain. http://www.hymnary.org/text/rock_of_ages_cleft_for_me_let_me_hide

CPSIA information can be obtained
at www.ICGtesting.com
Printed in the USA
LVHW04s1502130918
589970LV00001B/1/P